Dear George (Jeremy)

Thank you for your
prayers & support for
Louise & Me! We
love you both dearly.
May God bless you
en Profound Ways —

Jeff PS 91

"He Made the Stars Also"
Messianic Reflections

Dr. Jeffrey D. Johnson
Founder/Director
Israel Today Ministries
PO Box 522
Vista, CA 92085

Wipf and Stock Publishers
Eugene, Oregon

Wipf and Stock Publishers
199 West 8th Avenue, Suite 3
Eugene OR 97401
http://www/wipfandstock.com

ಇಂದಿ

"He Made the Stars Also"
Messianic Reflections
by Dr. Jeffrey D. Johnson
Copyright © 2003 by Dr. Jeffrey D. Johnson
ISBN: 1-59244-293-5

ಇಂದಿ

No claim is made for originality, as these studies
are a result of many years researching the Jewish roots
of Christianity and eschatology. The author is grateful
for the many sources made available to him—including the
bibliography to be found at the end of certain chapters.

ಇಂದಿ

The following articles were originally written by
Jeffrey D. Johnson in *Salvation Letter*,
International Ministries to Israel, Arlington Heights, IL:

Teshuvah—Repentance, June 1995
Shavuot: Feast of Pentecost, June 1996
Life, August 1995
Halakah—Walking the Walk, February 1995

The following articles were originally written by
Jeffrey D. Johnson in *Salvation*,
International Ministries to Israel, Arlington Heights, IL:

Things Future, January/February/March 1996
He made the Stars Also, July/August 1995
Seeing the Light, May/June 1995
Blessing, April/May/June 1996

All Scripture quotations are from the
King James Version of the Bible.

As husbands and fathers go, I have been extremely blessed. The Lord has given me two sons and a daughter-in-law who motivate me to attempt to walk what I talk. They are followers of God who have an immense passion for the Lord Jesus. Most of all, I am amazed at the Grace of God who bestows wonderful gifts upon His children. He also has given me the greatest gift; second only to salvation, in Louise, my wife of three decades. To her I dedicate this book. Louise, you are my life and inspiration in our pilgrim's journey and may we walk together with our Lord, and both hear the invitation of God to the marriage supper of the Lamb, where love will be perfected in eternity.

— Jeffrey

CONTENTS

PREFACE

To understand the Christian faith is to understand the original context. The Bible in which Christians base their beliefs is a Jewish book, written by Jewish men (with the exception of one or two) as they were moved by the Holy Spirit. The Messiah, in whom Christians put their faith and trust in, was of the seed of Abraham through Isaac, thus a Jewish Messiah. The Kingdom, in which Christians pray, "Thy Kingdom come," is nothing less than a Jewish Kingdom in which Jesus rules and reigns from Jerusalem for a thousand years.

Christians owe a debt to the Jew. Through the Jews came the Scriptures. Through the Jews came the Messiah, the Lord Jesus. Through the Jews came the Church.

How can the evangelical community begin to pay their debt they owe to Jewish people? *First of all*, by faithfully praying for them and the *"peace of Jerusalem"* (Psalm 122:6). *Secondly*, Christians need to learn salient points regarding Jewish culture in order to communicate effectively the message of the Messiah in a way that will be productive. *Finally*, Christians must learn to flesh out what they say they believe. In other words, walking the walk, rather, than just talking "religious" talk.

This being true, it would make sense for Christians to gain an understanding of the Jewish roots of their faith and belief. *"He Made the Stars Also"* addresses the Jewish Roots of Christianity covering various theological themes. This compilation of articles has circulated throughout the country with Dr. Johnson's *"Research Review"* and teaching letters. Pastors, bible teachers, Jewish people and Christians in general have benefited from these sound bites of pertinent information regarding Israel, prophecy and the Jewish roots of Christianity.

It is my hope that believers glean from this book helpful principles to redeem the time wisely because, *"time is short; life is precious & Jesus is coming soon."*

Until He comes, we are
Together Under His Wings,

Jeffrey D. Johnson

Founder/Director
Israel Today Ministries
PO Box 522
Vista, California 92085

1

The Hot Spot

W hen considering end-time events, we need to look at Israel. The current Middle East crisis is not a surprise to the student of the Bible. Events are unfolding exactly how the prophets said they would happen. To understand the key to all prophecy we need to examine one of the most sensitive pieces of property in the world today: Jerusalem!

In Zechariah chapter two we find the third of eight visions. Zechariah explains that there is to be a large increase in the size and population of Jerusalem. The context is future. The Millennium to be exact. In verse eight we find an eternal principle, "Those who touch Israel touch the pupil of God's eye." For over 3,000 years Jerusalem has been the capital of Israel. (Genesis 14:8; 22; Ezekiel 16:3; 1 Chronicles 11:4-9; 2 Chronicles 3:1)

God, allowing David to be victorious, gave Jerusalem to Israel, thus setting the stage for this city to be central in world events. Jewish sages fondly call Jerusalem the very center of the earth, even the universe. Jerusalem has been called the "lion of God," (Isaiah 29:1); "Joy," (Isaiah 65:18); "City of Truth," (Zechariah 8:3) "Throne of God," (Jeremiah 3:17). Everything that Christians and Jews hold dear comes from Jerusalem. Jerusalem is literally "the joy of the whole earth." (Psalm 48:2)

According to Scripture, Jerusalem is to be the capital of the world in the future. (Isaiah 2:2-4) However, the question is, "Who owns the land?"

The Muslim Palestinians say they own the land. Their argument stems from what is stated in the Koran (Sura 2:124-129) written centuries after Christ. You will read that Ishmael, Abraham's first-born, was bound on Moriah instead of Isaac as recorded in Genesis. Thus, Muslim Palestinians believe all the promises concerning the inheritance of the land go to the descendants of Ishmael (Arabs/Palestinians) instead of the descendants of Isaac (Jews). Therefore, the tension in the Middle East is a religious tension and family affair that started between the descendants of Ishmael and Isaac and Jacob and Esau. (Arabs also consider themselves descendants of Esau, Genesis 25).

The prophets stated that Israel would be restored in the last days, and subsequently Jerusalem would become a burden to the nations of the world (Amos 9:13-15; Zechariah 12:2,3). Ultimately, all nations will come against Israel through a sequence of events (Ezekiel 38,39; Zechariah 14:2; Joel 3:1,2). Finally, the Messiah will come. Jesus will return and establish His Kingdom on earth and rule and reign in Jerusalem (Psalm 132; Zechariah 14; Isaiah 2; Revelation 19; Matthew 6:10; Luke 1:33).

The Scripture outlines the tension between Arab and Jew. Unfortunately, bloodshed and ominous carnage is predicted (Ezekiel 38,39; Daniel 7-12). Even Iraq is mentioned (Jeremiah 50,51). However, the good news is that one day there will be peace. This peace will come when the Glory of Israel and the Light of the Gentiles returns. When Jesus returns we learn that there will be peace between Israel and the Arab nations (Isaiah 13:20-22; 19:23-25; Jeremiah 51:39-43; Ezekiel 47:13-48:29; Isaiah 34:5-10; 63:1-6; Isaiah 19:1-22).

The Scripture is replete with references to Israel in the context of end times. Even the tens of thousands of Jews who fled the former Soviet Union and came to Israel were foretold 2,500 years ago (Jeremiah 16:14,15). We live in exciting times! To summarize, the Scripture teaches:

1. Israel is to be restored as a nation in the last days.

2. Jerusalem will be the main point of tension regarding peace.

3. Arab nations, along with all the nations will ultimately come against Israel.

4. The Messiah will come and bring peace to all nations.

We are given a mandate regarding Jerusalem, *"Pray for the peace of Jerusalem"* (Psalm 122:6). Jesus taught us to pray "Thy Kingdom come." When you pray for the peace of Jerusalem and pray for Messiah's Kingdom to come, you are blessing Israel and petitioning God to bring peace.

Christian, understand that God is once again moving in the events of His ancient people Israel. Jerusalem is the "hot-spot" of world events. Jesus said, "When these things begin to happen, look up and lift up your heads, because your redemption draws near" (Luke 21:28).

2

Teshuvah—**Repentance**

Repent, and turn from all your transgressions, so
that iniquity will not be your ruin

— *Ezekiel* 18:30

When was the last time you heard a sermon on Sin and Repentance? Blaming others for our problems is a propensity that has become popular in some Christian circles. "Sin" and "Repentance" seemingly have been erased from our vocabulary and thinking process. What ever happened to accountability? I'm speaking of accountability to ourselves and especially to God?

"*Teshuvah*" is the Hebrew term for "Repentance." Jewish tradition teaches that repentance is motivated by two factors, namely, fear and love. Fear of the punishment from God and love for God. The Scripture is infused with the teaching of repentance and yet very little is said about this important doctrine. Jesus said, "except ye repent, ye shall all likewise perish" (Luke 13:3,5).

In Luke's Gospel we find an account of a woman, a "sinner," who heard that Jesus was near by. We read, "*And, behold, a woman in the city, which was a sinner, when she knew that Jesus sat at meat in the Pharisee's house, brought an alabaster box of ointment, and stood at his feet behind him weeping, and began to wash his feet with tears, and did wipe them with the hairs of her head, and kissed his feet, and anointed them with the ointment"* (Luke 7:37,38).

Please notice that she did not look into the face of our Lord. The awareness of her sin and His holiness was real which motivated her sense of humility. Trembling and weeping, wiping her tears with the hairs of her head she now begins to kiss his feet again and again anointing them with perfume. True repentance brings about genuine affection for God.

Jesus responded to her passion and sincerity as she turned from her sin by stating, *"Thy sins are forgiven...Thy faith hath saved thee; go in peace"* (verses 48,50).

Repentance is turning from sin, changing one's mind, understanding the necessity of knowing God. Just as this dear woman had an acute awareness of her sin and a need for the Savior, we too, must experience repentance that brings about the "New Birth" (John 3:3,7).

The Lord through the prophet Ezekiel (18:30-32) reminds us that we must *"Repent, and turn"* and *"Cast away"* our transgressions. Notice the phrases *"your transgressions;" "your ruin;" "turn and live."* This is why Jesus was *"wounded for our transgressions, He was bruised for our iniquities: the chastisement of our peace was upon Him; and with His stripes we are healed"* (Isaiah 53:5).

Let us not lose sight of the reality of "Sin" and the need for "Repentance" in this age of "psychobabble." With the woman in Luke 7 in mind, let us take to heart the truth of our Lord's words: *"Come unto me, all ye that labor and are heavy laden, and I will give you rest. Take my yoke upon you, and learn of me; for I am meek and lowly in heart: and ye shall find rest unto your souls. For my yoke is easy, and my burden is light"* (Matthew 11:28-30).

3

Things Future

Paul expresses to young Timothy, "that in the last days *perilous times shall come*" (2 Timothy 3:1, "perilous" implying "demoni-cally fierce"). In verses 2 through 9 he describes a complete societal breakdown of morals, laws and absolutes. The characteristic of the world that surrounds the Church does not reflect a betterment of civilization, but rather the opposite (Luke 17:26-30; 18:8). In fact, we must remember the "world" doesn't want the Church here, and the propensity of fallen man is to do the opposite of what God teaches and mirror disobedience rather than obedience (John 15:18-20; Ephesians 2:2,3). The Christian's hope does not rest in the political endeavor for global uniformity and peace. Rather, the Christian rests in *"that blessed hope, and the glorious appearing of the great God and our Savior, Jesus Christ"* (Titus 2:13). We understand *"that day shall not come, except there come a falling away first"* (2 Thessalonians 2:3).

The actual time of the Lord's literal return on the earth, which is called the "Second Advent," will happen at the end of the seven-year Tribulation Period. The "Rapture" (from the Latin *"rapio"* meaning "caught up") will happen seven years before the Second Advent and can unfold at anytime. This is the mysterious and miraculous catching away or disappearance of believers in Christ, those in the grave and those alive on earth, as they meet the Lord in the air (John 14:1-3; 1 Thessalonians 4:13-18; 1 Corinthians 15:51-52; Revelation 4:1).

In fact, no one knows the day or the hour the rapture will take place (Matthew 24:36; 25:13; Mark 13:32,33; Luke 12:35-40; Acts 1:7).There are *no signs* regarding the Rapture of the Church. The Rapture is imminent (Acts 1:11; 1 Corinthians 15:51,52; Philippians 3:20; Colossians 3:4; 1 Thessalonians 1:10; 1 Timothy 6:14; James 5:8). *Signs* are indicators for Israel during the Tribulation or *"Time of Jacob's Trouble"* attesting that their *"redemption draweth nigh"* (Luke 21:28; Joel 2:1,2,11; 3:11-16; Matthew 24; Daniel 9:27; Revelation 4-19). The so-called signs, shadows and thundering we see today on the horizon are very real, but are pointing toward *Tribulation* events and ultimately the Second Advent...not the Rapture.

In this day, where many false teachers, sensationalists, and "feel good" ministries exist, we must remain faithful to the text of Scripture *"rightly dividing the word of truth"* (2 Timothy 2:15). *"For the time will come when they will not endure sound doctrine; but after their own lust shall they heap to themselves teachers, having itching ears; and they shall turn away their ears from the truth, and shall be turned unto fables"* (2 Timothy 4:3,4).

For a clear understanding of "Things Future" here is a brief synopsis (*not all inclusive*) of events yet to unfold:

1. *Rapture* (John 14:3; 1 Corinthians 15:51,52; Thessalonians 4:13-18; Revelation 4:1): This event is imminent. There are no signs preceding the Rapture and it will happen seven years before the Second Advent. Immediately after the Rapture, the *"Judgment Seat of Christ"* takes place (2 Corinthians 5:10). This is a judgment for believers (those who are saved) in order to determine eternal rewards, or lack of rewards, based upon obedience.

2. *Tribulation Period* or *"Time of Jacob's Trouble"* (Isaiah 26:20; Daniel 9:26,27; 12:1; Matthew 24; Luke 21:25; 1 Thessalonians 5:1-8; Revelation 4-19): The Tribulation lasts for seven years and will take place after the Rapture of the Church. The Antichrist will come on the scene and create a treaty of peace in the Middle East that affects the world for three and one half years. During the second half of the Tribulation, the Antichrist will show his "true colors" as Satan

incarnate, on the Earth and break the treaty, and declare himself Messiah.

Jesus said this would be a time of *"great tribulation, such as was not since the beginning of the world to this time, no nor ever shall be"* (Matthew 24:21). God's wrath will be poured out upon the earth during this time. The Battle of Gog and Magog will culminate during the middle part of the Tribulation (Ezekiel 38,39). Then, the Battle of Armageddon will mark the beginning of the end of the Tribulation (Zechariah 14:1-3; Revelation 16:13-16; 19:11-21). Also, "Commercial" and "Religious" Babylon will be destroyed probably towards the end of the Tribulation (Jeremiah 50,51; Isaiah 13,14; Revelation 17,18).

3. *Second Advent* (Zechariah 14:4,5; Matthew 24:29-31; Revelation 19:11-21): This is when the Lord literally comes to earth. He defeats the armies of the Antichrist on the plain of Megiddo. He casts Satan into the *"Bottomless Pit"* for one thousand years and Jesus the Messiah will rule the earth from the Throne of David in the golden eternal city of Jerusalem. The curse will be removed from the earth and those who believed in Messiah will begin to reign with Him, for He is the *King of Kings* and *Lord of Lords* (Isaiah 11:1-10; Daniel 2:44; Luke 19:11-27; Romans 8:18-23; Revelation 20:1-6).

At this time the nation Israel will come to know that Jesus is indeed the Messiah and believe on Him. What a glorious day that will be! Until this event takes place there will be a *"remnant"* of God's ancient people that will come to believe in Jesus as Messiah (Romans 11:5; Isaiah 11:10-12:6; Jeremiah 30:7-11; Ezekiel 20:33-38; Zechariah 12:8-10; 13:6; 14:16-21; Romans 11:25-29).

Also, the *"Sheep-Goat Judgment"* will take place during this time (Matthew 25:31-46), meaning, the Gentile nations will be judged based on their treatment of the Jews during the Tribulation.

4. *Satan's Final Revolt* (Revelation 20:7-15): Satan will be released after the thousand years and he will try one more time to overthrow God. He will not succeed. He will be cast into the *"Lake of Fire"* for eternity.

5. *Great White Throne* (Revelation 20:11-15): This is the final judgment for those who have rejected God's message of redeeming grace through Messiah Jesus, our Lord. At this time the earth will be destroyed (2 Peter 3).

6. *New Heaven, New Earth, New Jerusalem* (2 Peter 3:7-13; Revelation 21,22): God shall wipe away all tears. There will be no more death, pain, sorrow or crying. God will make all things new. Then, we will enter the eternal state abiding with God (Ephesians 2:7; 2Peter 1:11; Revelation 11:15).

This is our hope! This is our assurance!

So, in the final analysis, we are not looking for signs. We are looking for the glorious appearing of our Lord and Savior Messiah Jesus. We are to bring people to a saving knowledge of the Lord. We are to live godly in an ungodly world and be faithful until our Lord returns. We are to comfort one another with this blessed hope (Matthew 28:19,20; Acts 1:8; 2 Peter 3:11,14; Titus 2:12,13; 1 Thessalonians 3:13; 5:23; Hebrews 10:25; 1 Thessalonians 4:18).

4

Halakah—Walking the Walk

He hath shewed thee, O man, what is good; and what doth
the Lord require of thee, but to do justly, and to love
mercy, and to walk humbly with thy God.

— *Micah* 6:8.

This verse reflects what some call the *"Jewish Golden Rule"* and is
termed *"Halakah."* Halakah is the quintessential characteristic of
Judaism.[1] The word Halakah is derived from the Hebrew word for
"walking." Not only is Halakah the legal part of the Talmud, it is the way
a "religious" Jew lives out his faith. By following rules of conduct as
described in the Bible, as interpreted by the rabbis (i.e., Ten Commandments, circumcision, keeping Shabbat, keeping kosher, etc.), religious
Jews believe the "Holy One" will be pleased and accept them eternally.
In essence, the Halakah is the path that the Jew must follow throughout
his life.[2] Halakah has been the instrument by which Judaism has
expressed its theology and morality.[3]

The early church reflected this concept of Halakah. For example, the
Apostle John wrote, *"He that saith he abideth in Him ought himself also
so to walk, even as He walked"* (1 John 2:6). Also, Paul wrote to the

Ephesians explaining how the Christian ought to walk in chapters 4,5,6. He addresses unity, compassion, holiness, truthfulness, obedience and so on. In one chapter he writes, *"Be ye therefore followers* (or imitators) *of God...and walk in love, as Christ also hath loved us..."* (Ephesians 5:1,2). Eight times in Ephesians Paul uses the word "walk" which means "to walk around" or "to order ones behavior." This is the idea of Halakah.

Early Church Fathers also understood Halakah. Polycarp, a disciple of the Apostle John wrote, *"...we must gird on the armour of integrity, and the first step must be to school our own selves into conformity with the Divine commandments."*[4] In the first century, Ignatius of Antioch declared, "...do not have Jesus Christ on your lips, and the world in your heart."[5] With reference to the Christian's lifestyle, Francis of Assisi in the early 13th century stated, *"Preach the gospel at all times. If necessary, use words."*

We find in Romans 11:11 that, *"...salvation is come unto the Gentiles, for to provoke them (the Jews) to jealousy."* The natural question would be, "What would cause them to be jealous?" First of all, anyone, Jew or Gentile, would be jealous of:

1. The security that comes from the hope and peace a believer has in Jesus (Romans 5:1-11).

2. The love that is manifested between those who believe (Galatians 5:22,23).

3. Life—your life, your Halakah, will speak louder than any words you say.

"Walking the Walk" will provoke both Jew and Gentile to jealousy. As one dear Jewish man stated, "I've read the New Testament and I like the Jesus of the Gospels...however, I do not like the Jesus I see in the churches." My dear Christian reader, what are we showing those around us? Are we "walking the walk" (Halakah) or are we simply talking a good talk? May God help us to imitate the "Jesus of the Gospels" in our lives.

Shalom!

Notes

1. Phillip Sigal, "Judaism, The Evolution of a Faith," (Grand Rapids, Eerdmans, 1988) p. 1.

2. Rabbi Dr. Shmuel Himelstein, "The Jewish Primer, Questions and Answers on the Jewish Faith and Culture," (Facts on File The Jerusalem Publishing House, 1990), p. 12.

3. Phillip Sigal, "Judaism, The Evolution of a Faith," (Grand Rapids, Eerdmans, 1988), p. 3.

4. Maxwell Staniforth, "Early Christian Writings, The Apostolic Fathers," (Penquin Books, 1984), p. 145.

5. Ibid., 106.

5

Seeing the Light

Light plays an important role in some religious traditions. For example, in the tradition of Judaism lighting candles on Shabbat is to remind Jewish people of their Creator and to set apart this day from other days. Also, lighting the Hanukkah menorah is a memorial of the miracle of God's intervention on Israel's behalf in 168 B.C. Plus, the seven branch menorah found in the synagogue and formerly in the Temple "tells of an eternal light of divine origin, but tended by man." [1] It is stated that this "holy lamp bore light in the Temple and from there to the world." [2] Even the "light" from Genesis 1:3, which was in existence before the luminaries (verses 14-19), "was a light, according to the [rabbinical] sages, set aside for the future of Messianic fulfillment." [3]

All these symbols point to God in one way or another. Unfortunately, many are blinded to the full meaning of the "Light." The Apostle Paul stated, *"But even unto this day, when Moses is read, the veil is upon their heart"* (2 Corinthians 3:15).

"Light" in scripture is usually synonymous with God, hope, the "written" Word, or the "living" Word (Jesus). For example, we find in the Gospel of Luke, as the angelic announcement came to the shepherds concerning Christ's birth, that *"the glory of the Lord shone round about them…"* (Luke 2:9). The *"glory"* was this brilliant eternal light that terrified the shepherds as they realized they were in the presence of the Holy. Also, when Joseph and Mary entered the Temple with the baby

Jesus in order to fulfill the custom of the Law, (sacrifice for Mary's purification 40 days after the birth of a son), *"a just and devout"* man took the baby up in his arms and stated that Jesus is *"A **light** to lighten the Gentiles, and the **glory** of thy people Israel"* (Luke 2:32).

Jesus said, *"I am the **light** of the world: he that followeth Me shall not walk in darkness, but shall have the **light** of life"* (John 8:12).

"Darkness" describes the condition of a person's heart. One will stumble in the darkness unless they have a light to guide their way. Tradition, though beautiful, is not the "light." Religion, though commendable, is not the "light." Self-esteem and self-awareness, though important, is not the 'light." The psalmist wrote, *"Thy word is a lamp unto my feet, and a light unto my path"* (Psalm 119:105). He found the secret to "dispel the darkness", namely, the Word of God. The Apostle John stated, *"In the beginning was the Word, and the Word was with God, and the Word was God...and the Word was made flesh, and dwelt among us"* (John 1:1,14).

Jesus, the Living Word, is the "Light" that dispels the darkness of sin from your heart. He is the "Passover Lamb," the one without spot or blemish, the perfect sacrifice on Calvary for the sins of the world. You see, without the shedding of blood there is no remission of sin (Hebrews 9:22). This is why Jesus had to die on the Cross and rise again.

Jesus Christ is *"the true Light, which lighteth every man that cometh into the world"* (John 1:9). The reason people do not come to the Light is *"there are insensitive hearts, still incapable of receiving this Light because the weight of their sins prevents them from seeing it. Let them not imagine that the Light is absent because they do not see it, for on account of their sins they are in darkness. 'And the light shineth in darkness; and the darkness comprehended it not' (John 1:5). Therefore...like the blind man exposed to the sun, the sun being present to him but he being absent from the sun, so the insensitive one, the sinner, the impious has a blind heart"* [4] —Augustine (354-430 AD).

Let us therefore examine our hearts to see if we are walking in the "Light" or walking in darkness. Do you know the Lord Jesus Christ as your personal Savior, or are you still walking in the darkness of darkness? Come to the Light and receive eternal life!

"Believe on the Lord Jesus Christ, and thou shalt be saved" (Acts 16:31).

Notes

1. Leo Trepp, *"A History of the Jewish Experience,"* (Behrman House, Inc., New York, 1973), p. 203.

2. Benjamin Blech, *"More Secrets of Hebrew Words,"* (Jason Aronson, Inc., New Jersey, 1993), p. 17.

3. Benjimin Blech, *"The Secrets of Hebrew Words,"* (Jason Aronson Inc., New Jersey, 1991), p. 30.

4. Mary T. Clark, *"Augustine of Hippo,"* (Paulist Press, New Jersey, 1984), p. 280.

6

He Made the Stars Also

What an awesome thought to ponder as you consider the billions of stars that exist. These five words reflect the sovereign creative ability of *God* (Hebrew, *"Elohim"*, making reference to His majestic power). The phrase, *"He made the stars also,"* is like an after-thought, *"Oh, by the way, God* (Elohim) *created the stars also."* Wow!

From time to time, we need to be reminded that God is sovereign and has a plan for the universe and specifically your life. The prophet Isaiah reminds us, *"Thus saith God the Lord, He that created the heavens, and stretched them out; He that spread forth the earth, and that which cometh out of it; He that giveth breath unto the people upon it, and spirit to them that walk therein: I, the Lord have called thee in righteousness, and will hold thine hand, and will keep thee..." (Isaiah 42:5,6).*

We can see in these verses that God has great concern and truly cares for His people. If God can create *"the stars also"* in all their glory and magnificence, can He not care for your concerns and needs? Listen to the words of David as he asks, *"What is man, that Thou art mindful of him? And the son of man, that Thou visitest him? For Thou hast made him a little lower than the angels, and hast crowned him with glory and honor"* (Psalm 8:4,5).

The term, *"mindful"* suggests that God is continually thinking about man. We are constantly on His mind. He has crowned those who trust in Him with glory and honor. One day believers in Jesus will be His trophies of Grace eternally displayed before all creation (Ephesians 2:7). Also, David states, with extreme pathos, *"I am poor and needy; yet the Lord thinketh upon me: Thou art my help and my deliverer; make no tarrying, O my God"* (Psalm 40:17).

The word "thinketh" (thinks) has the idea 'to regard and value.' Just as the parent or grandparent that carries photos of their children or grandchildren ready to show them at any moment. Constantly in the back of their mind, they are cherishing and regarding their "kids" or "grandkids." So it is with God and his children…He *thinks* upon us.

Be not afraid dear one, *"for in Him we live and move and have our being."* The Lord Jesus will never leave us nor forsake us. We are *"complete in Him'* who is *"all and in all"* (Acts 17:28; Hebrews 13:5; Colossians 2:10; 3:11).

Therefore, rest in the confidence that He who *"made the stars also"* can complete that which He has started in you and will hold your hand; and keep you along the journey. Amen and Amen!

7

Battle of Gog & Magog

In the book of Ezekiel we find a prophecy regarding a fierce battle that will take place in the end of time. In fact, many theologians believe that it will culminate during the 7-year Tribulation period of the world. This battle is generally called the "Battle of Gog and Magog." The prophet lists a coalition of nations and a leader of this coalition. However, the exact location of some of these nations is debated. Nevertheless, we have a good idea as to what will take place in the future regarding these nations.

In chapters 36 & 37 Ezekiel reveals to us the miraculous regathering and restoration of Israel in the last days. Chapters 38 & 39 describe a horrible battle that takes place against the restored nation. The reason for this battle, according to the prophets, is that Israel, especially Jerusalem, will become the center of attention for the world in the latter days.

Ezekiel outlines the coalition of nations that come against Israel. We learn that God intervenes and Israel is gloriously saved from utter destruction. However, there is great carnage as a result of this battle. The question before us in this article is, "Who are these nations and why will they attack Israel?"

The answer as to why they come against Israel is found in verses 10-12 of chapter 38. There will be a time when Israel believes she is dwelling in safety and relative peace. Her walls of defense are down and she is duped into believing that all is well. (This could very well be because of the treaty created by the Antichrist, Daniel 9:27).

Let us take look at this coalition of nations:

1. *Magog* (verse 2): References the territory that is located in Southern Russia around the Black Sea. Other historians say that Magog refers also to parts of southern Europe. Magog was a son of Japheth (Gen. 10:2; 1 Chron. 1:5). **Gog** (verse 2): refers to the leader of this coalition.

2. *Chief Prince* (verse 2): The Hebrew word for "Chief" is *"Rosh."* Better translated, "Prince of Rosh." Some scholars say that "Rosh" refers to Russia.

3. *Meshech* and *Tubal* (verse 2): These were also sons of Japheth (Gen. 10:2). They settled in an area that today is called Turkey. These descendants also settled the eastern parts of Europe and southern Russia. Some suggest that Meshech refers to the area surrounding modern day Moscow and that Tubal refers to the area of modern day Tobolsk. However, it can be a stretch to give modern names to Meshech and Tubal because they sound similar to these two modern day cities. In the time of Ezekiel this area would have been in and around Turkey.

4. *Persia* (verse 5): Iran (from the east).

5. *Ethiopia* (verse 5): (from the south).

6. *Libya* (verse 5): (from the west).

7. *Gomer/Togarmah* (verse 6): Northern & Eastern Turkey (from the north).

8. *Sheba/Dedan* (verse 13): Arabian Peninsula. They will seemingly protest the battle.

9. *Tarshish* (verse 13): Refers to the western part of the Mediterranean area. Tarshish will also protest the attack.

Those nations that attack Israel will be defeated as God intervenes. Some believe, with this coalition out of the way the Antichrist will make his move and gain his maximum control over the world.

As we consider this prophesy we understand that the possibility of such a war is not beyond modern day scope. Knowing that one day a coalition of nations surrounding Israel, led by a leader from the north, will attempt to overthrow her, we should pray for Israel and assist her in any way possible. May God help us to bless Israel! (Gen. 12:1-3)

Time is short, Life is precious and Jesus is coming soon!

8

Where Will the Baby or Young Child Go if He/She Should Die?

First of all, the bible does not speak directly on this issue. Some suggest this may be on purpose in order not to give cultists a license for infanticide to guarantee their children's salvation. On one hand, babies and children are not ensured of heaven because of "sinlessness" or "innocence." All have sinned, even babies.

David stated, "*Behold, I was shapen in iniquity, and in sin did my mother conceive me.*" (Psalm 51:5)

Paul said it this way, "*Wherefore, as by one man sin entered into the world and death by sin; and so death passed upon all men, for that all have sinned.*" (Romans 5:12)

"*For all have sinned*" (Romans 3:23) means, because Adam sinned, we all have sinned, even babies. So a baby needs salvation, just as an adult. On the other hand, the Lord's death on the cross delivers us from sin.

In the Old Testament, particularly in the Book of Leviticus, you have offerings that typify Messiah's sacrifice for sin. For example, the "sin-offering" (Leviticus 4), known also as the "guilt-offering", gives us the understanding that Jesus' death guarantees deliverance from our fallen nature, from sins intentional or unintentional.

The "trespass-offering" (Leviticus 5), declares that the Messiah's death on the cross provides forgiveness for every evil thought, word, and deed we commit against Him. We are accountable for our sins, and yet, by God's grace, through the shed blood of our Lord we find mercy and forgiveness.

Therefore, a baby would receive forgiveness on the basis of the sin-offering. Christ, the last Adam, shed His blood for us, removing the penalty for all sins, unintentional or intentional. However, when a child becomes accountable, knowing right from wrong, understanding what sin is, and why Jesus died for our sins, he or she needs to be saved. This means they are now accountable and need to receive or reject the gospel.

Let's explore this further. David implied that a baby would depart to be with God. When his child died we read these words, *"While the child was yet alive, I fasted and wept: for I said, who can tell whether God will be gracious to me, that the child may live? But now he is dead, wherefore should I fast? Can I bring him back again? I shall go to him, but he shall not return to me. And David comforted Bathsheba his wife"* (2 Sam. 12:22-24).

You see David knew that there was existence after death. David believed in God and knew that He would see His child again. The implication is clear. Jesus said, *"Suffer (permit) little children, and forbid them not, to come unto me: for of such is the kingdom of heaven"* (Matt. 19:14). This does not directly address the issue of where a baby goes when they die. However, the passage gives us an insight to the compassion of our Lord accepting the children into His bosom.

In the final analysis, all have a sin nature, even babies, because of Adam's sin. Christ, the second Adam, became sin for us on the cross. Babies and young children unknowingly partake of the curse of the first Adam. Therefore, they unknowingly partake of the redemption of the second Adam. Meaning when a baby or a very young child dies, they are saved through the shed blood of our Lord Jesus. Jesus being our sin offering took away the guilt and condemnation of sin. It is not until that child comes to an age of accountability, knowing right and wrong, sin and non-sin, that he or she would need to make a personal decision, accepting or rejecting Jesus as their Messiah and Savior.

I pray that this brings comfort and blessing. Praise be to God for His mercy, love and grace through Jesus our beloved Savior!

9

The Jewish Interpretation
of Prophecy

Rabbi Harold Kushner tells a story of a little boy who came home from Sunday School and his mother asked him what he had learned that day. He told her, *"The Israelites got out of Egypt, but Pharaoh and his army chased after them. They got to the Red Sea and couldn't cross it and the Egyptian army was getting closer. So Moses got on his walkie-talkie, the Israeli air force bombed the Egyptians, and the Israeli navy built a pontoon bridge so the people could cross."* The mother was very astonished and asked, *"Is that the way they taught you the story?"* The little boy answered, *"Well no, but if I told you what they told us, you'd never believe it."* [1]

This is also true when you think about the modern nation Israel. It is amazing to realize that thousands of years ago biblical prophets foretold the restoration of this nation. This is nothing less than a miracle and is unprecedented in the history of man, that a people, who were dispersed throughout all the nations, would return over 2,000 years later. In fact in 1998 Israel celebrated their Year of Jubilee that of 50 years of miraculous restoration.

In eons past, God created the world, the planets and the stars. The climax of the Lord's creation was man. Nearly 4,000 years ago God chose a 75 year-old man from Mesopotamia named Abraham and made a covenant with him. Abraham lived 300 years after the flood and Jewish tradition declares that his mother took him as a child to learn from Noah & Shem.

When the Lord made this covenant (Genesis 12:1-3) He began to communicate through Abraham's progeny. Through Abraham came the promised son, Isaac, then Jacob, the 12 patriarchs, Moses, the judges, kings and prophets. The Lord conveyed a story of an Anointed One that would come, a Messiah who would redeem Israel and deliver them from their oppressors. He also disclosed a promise concerning land that exclusively belongs to the descendants of Isaac. This hope touched the very soul within the children of Israel.

This promise of real-estate has become the most percolative issue throughout the millennia. *Who owns the land?* This question is the main issue regarding the Middle East. It is a religious issue, not political. The descendants of Isaac say they own the land. The descendants of Ishmael say the land belongs to them. Both Isaac (Jews) and Ishmael (Arabs) are children of Abraham. The Jew's claim to the land is found within the writings of Scripture. The Arab's claim to the land is found in the writings of the Koran (Sura 2:124-129) where they believe that Abraham bound Ishmael, not Isaac, on the altar. Thus, they believe all the promises of inheritance and blessing would fall upon the descendants of Ishmael, the first-born of Abraham.

With this brief introduction, let's now look at the Jewish Interpretation of Prophecy and the Middle East addressing three areas: The Land, the Messiah, & The Kingdom.

The Land

It is understood that Sir Moses Montefiore, a Jew, purchased a piece of property near Jerusalem. He was the first Jew, in over 1200 years, to own property in what would become, Israel. That was over a century ago. Today, the State of Israel celebrates over 5 decades of existence. Jewish people own *"Eretz Yisrael,"*—the land of Israel. Scripture is replete with references of the land promise given to the descendants of Isaac and particularly the physical restoration in the later days.

In Amos chapter 9, God says of Israel, *"I will raise up his ruins, and I will build it as in the days of old...And I will bring again the captivity of my people of Israel and they shall build the waste cities, and inhabit them; and they shall plant vineyards, and drink the wine thereof; they shall also make gardens, and eat the fruit of them. And I will plant them upon their land, and they shall no more be pulled up out of their land which I have given them, saith the Lord thy God." (vss. 11,14,15)*

In 1897, the First Zionist Congress met in Basel, Switzerland. The main personality was Dr. Theodore Herzl. He declared that one day, a Jewish state, a homeland would exist for the children of Israel.

Fifty years later, after the horrors of the holocaust, the UN voted Israel into existence so that the Jews could have a homeland of their own. The year was 1947. On May 14, 1948, the British lowered their flags at 8:00 A.M. in Jerusalem. Six Arab nations responded by declaring war against the newly formed State of Israel. Ben Gurion, Israel's first Prime Minister, at 4:00 P.M., declared to the world, that the state of Israel was born. God has subsequently protected Israel through the many attacks, wars and terrorist threats throughout these last 50 years. What the prophets predicted has come true. Israel is once again back in their land. *"And I will plant them upon their land, and they shall no more be pulled up out of their land which I have given them..."*

Twenty-six hundred years ago, the prophet Ezekiel foretold Israel's restoration. In chapter 37, he saw a valley that was full of dry bones signifying that life was gone from them. Ezekiel was perplexed at this frightful scene that was before him. God asked the prophet, *"Can these bones live?"* He answered, *"O Lord God, thou knowest."* Ezekiel answered wisely and God commanded the prophet to prophecy and say to these bones in the valley of death, *"Hear the word of the Lord... ye shall live...and ye shall know that I am the Lord."*

God gave the interpretation of this strange prophecy:

1. Israel's hope is diminished (verse 11, *the Diaspora*).
2. Israel will be restored to the land (Chapters 36,37).
3. Israel will first return in unbelief (verse 8, no breath in them).
4. Israel will then believe (verses 9,10,14).

Israel has completed the first three stages of this prophecy. It is interesting to note that the "Tanach," the Jewish Bible (same as the Christian Old Testament, however, the books are in different order) ends with the book of 2 Chronicles and the story of Cyrus. After defeating the Babylonians, Cyrus gives the Jews opportunity to return to Jerusalem to rebuild their Temple. Second Chronicles ends with the Hebrew word *"Aliyah" meaning to* "go up." Today it means "to go live in Israel."

During the last 50 years, hundreds of thousands of Jews have made their "Aliyah" just as the prophets declared. O beloved, the **Word of God is true!** It is interesting to note that the New Testament also ends with the thought of "Aliyah," a greater aliyah. In Revelation 4:1 the Lord speaks to John and says, *"Come up hither"* (come up here) which is the Greek word, *"anabaino"* which means "to go up." This is a typological figure of the rapture of the Church. My friend, be sure you are ready to meet the Lord.

The fourth stage of Israel's restoration will not unfold until the Messiah returns at the conclusion of the Tribulation Period (Zechariah 14:4). Israel will then become fully restored spiritually as a nation and believe in Messiah Jesus (Ezekiel 37:14). Until that glorious day, there will be a remnant that will be saved during the present church age (Romans 11:5).

One final thought concerning the complete restoration of Israel. *"And I will pour upon the house of David, and upon the inhabitants of Jerusalem, the spirit of grace and of supplications; and they shall look upon me whom they have pierced ... "* (Zechariah 12:10).

In Zechariah's prophecy we find that the word *"whom"* is comprised of two Hebrew letters, the aleph & tav, the first and the last letters of the Hebrew alphabet. Therefore, implying the One described in this verse, is the *"first and the last,"* the *"beginning and the end",* the "totality" regarding all Jewish expectation of Messiah. This One that Israel will see is the *"Alpha and Omega,"* (the first and last letters of the Greek alphabet), namely, "Yeshua HaMeshiach,"—Jesus the Messiah. What a glorious day that will be when Israel beholds and believes in Jesus the Messiah.

"And it shall be said in that day: 'Lo, this is our God; We have waited for Him... " Isaiah 5:9.

The Messiah

A Jewish woman, who attended my former bible studies in the Chicago suburbs, was stunned at an Old Testament riddle:

Who hath ascended up into heaven, or descended?
Who hath gathered the wind in his first?
Who hath bound the waters in a garment?
Who hath established all the ends of the earth?
What is his name, and what is his son's name,
if thou canst tell? Proverbs 30:4

She blurted out, *"I know his name! I know who he is! It must be JESUS!"* She put her hand over her mouth and with a surprised look on her face, declared, *"What shall I do? I am not supposed to believe this!"*

For thousands of years, the Jewish people have been waiting for the Anointed One, the Messiah of Israel, a Prophet like Moses and the Prince of Peace. There are at least forty-eight main prophecies regarding the Messiah. One scientist stated the chance of all these prophecies happening arbitrarily is 1 in 10 to the power of 157. That is the number 10 followed by 157 zeroes. Yet it happened in the person of Jesus of Nazareth.

A remnant of Jews believe in Jesus as Paul stated in Romans 11:5. In fact, it is estimated today that approximately 1 in 20 Jewish people believe that Jesus is the Messiah. In the January 1994 issue of the Jerusalem Post (and in other issues) an advertisement entitled, *"The Jewish Response to Missionaries"* asked this question, *"What are we doing wrong? And what are they doing right? Why have more Jews converted to Christianity in the last 19 years that in the last 1900 years?"* Jewish people, by the thousands, are coming to faith in Messiah!

What have Jewish people said about Jesus?

…I am enthralled by the luminous figure of the Nazarene…No one can read the Gospels without feeling the actual presence of Jesus. His personality pulsates in every word. No myth is filled with such life. Albert Einstein, *Saturday Evening Post*, October, 1929[2]

Solomon B. Freehof, former professor of medieval liturgy and rabbinics, Hebrew Union College, Cincinnati, 1915-1924.

"Jesus of Nazareth is the most famous name in the world...The significant fact is that time has not faded the vividness of his image. Poetry still sings his praise. He is still the living comrade of countless lives. No Moslem ever sings, 'Mohammed, lover of my soul,' nor does any Jew say of Moses, the teacher, 'I need thee every hour'." [3]

So why don't Jewish people believe in Jesus as Messiah?

What do some religious Jewish scholars believe about the Messiah of Israel?

First of all, the rabbis teach that the Messiah will be a redeemer for Israel, one who will bring peace. He will not be God-man, meaning He will not be divinity in human flesh. They are looking for a mighty prince like David, a King of nations, a great teacher and a mighty deliverer.

Secondly, the Jewish sages believe in *two messiahs* or two redeemers. Messiah Ben (son of) Joseph, and Messiah Ben (son of) David. Ben Joseph will have an important role as he will lead the armed forces of Israel in battle during the Tribulation, probably associated with the Battle of Gog and Magog, (Ezekiel 38,39; Obadiah 18) in which He will be killed. As a result Israel will experience great trial and tribulation. Shortly thereafter, Messiah Ben David will appear and avenge Ben Joseph's death, and in fact *resurrect him* from the dead and make him viceroy in His kingdom. This will begin the *Messianic era* of religious and political peace. (for further study see, *Mashiach, The Principle of Mashiach and the Messianic Era in Jewish Law and Tradition*, by Jacob Immanuel Schochet, S.I.E. Publishing, 1992).

It seems that the main function of Ben Joseph is to prepare the way for Ben David to come with glory and power in order to establish the Messianic Kingdom.

There are some interesting parallels regarding the Jewish definition of the two messiahs and what is written in the Book of Revelation.

Notice that Ben Joseph will be:

1. A world viceroy or political leader
2. A Military Dignitary
3. Initiator/facilitator of peace and religious reform

4. Killed and resurrected

The Anti-Christ will also be:

1. A world viceroy or political leader (Daniel 8:23; 11:36)
2. A Military Dignitary (Revelation 6:2; 13:2; 17:11,12)
3. An initiator/facilitator of peace and religious reform (Revelation 13:8,16; Daniel 11:36,37; 2 Thessalonians 2:3,4)
4. Killed and resurrected (Revelation 13:2,3,11,12)

In verses 11 & 12 of Revelation chapter thirteen we find that *"another beast"* appears on the scene after the Anti-Christ is killed. Although this "beast", which is the "False Prophet", does not actually resurrect the Anti-Christ, he is a witness to it and encourages the world to follow after him as the Messiah. Therefore, we have **"two" key personalities** or "two redeemers", "two Messiahs."

Please understand the Jewish sages did not consult the Book of Revelation for information. The Evil One is preparing the world for the great deception that is to come.

The Kingdom

In pondering the truths of the book of Revelation, church historian Eusebius (263-339 AD) stated regarding his perplexity,

> For, though I do not understand, yet I suspect that some deeper sense is enveloped in the words, and these I do not measure and judge by my private reason; but allowing more to faith, I have regarded them as too lofty to comprehended by me, and those things which I do not understand, I do not reject, but I wonder the more that I cannot comprehend. (Book VII, Chapter XXV, *The Apocalypse of John*)

As we look at the *"Olam Ha-Ba"* (Hebrew for *the Age to come*) may we realize that Israel is the key to understanding prophecy. All prophecies are centered around God's dealings with His ancient people Israel. One day Messiah Jesus will return descending upon the Mount of Olives and begin His Kingdom taking His rightful place upon David's Throne. (Zechariah 12-14)

On that day Israel will say:

This is our God; we have waited for him, and he will save us: this is the Lord; we have waited for him, we will be glad and rejoice in his salvation. Isaiah 25:9

Israel longs for *"yemoth hamashiah"* or the "days of the Messiah." This will be an age of universal peace and harmony between nations. A time of prosperity and justice. A utopia will unfold under the leadership of Messiah.

What the Rabbis say.

The rabbis say the peoples of the world will flock to Israel and convert to Judaism embracing the God of Abraham, Isaac and Jacob. It will be a time where Torah is observed, studied and cherished.

Also they say this utopia will be prefaced by great calamities, wars, turmoil and human suffering, specifically Israel's suffering and that the war of Gog and Magog will precede the Days of Messiah. The rabbinic sages believe that in the *seventh millennium* messianic peace and the "reign of God" will come to pass. Thus, messianic expectation is at an all-time high among the religious Jews in Israel because it is believed that the 21st century may be the beginning of the seventh millennium. The rabbis believe the Days of Messiah will also be a time where the teachings of the Torah will guide the nations to the knowledge of "Ancient of Days," the God of Israel. Thus, you have the catalyst for world peace. (see, *The Universal Jewish Encyclopedia, Messianic Era*)

What the Scriptures say.

Beloved, when Jesus returns He will indeed fulfill all these expectations of the Jewish sages and more. The "Lamb of God" will become the "Lion of Judah" (Genesis 49:9; Revelation 5:5). Sin will be forgiven (Hebrews 9:28), Satan will be bound (Revelation 20:2) and *Yeshua* (Hebrew way of saying Jesus) will rule and reign for one thousand years (Revelation 20:4). Oh, what a glorious day that will be!

The *"aharit ha-yammin"* or the "end of time" is real. The *"yemoth hamashiah"* or "days of Messiah" will happen. The Messianic Era will bring a complete change to the dynamic of human behavior unprecedented since the age of Adam and Eve in Eden.

In conclusion, the Jews are returning to the land, as the prophets declared. There is great anticipation among many Jewish sages regarding the coming of Messiah and the Messianic Kingdom in the seventh millennium.

The Scripture teaches that no one will know the day or hour Jesus the Messiah will return. However, we are commanded to watch and be faithful. God truly cares and wants us to understand that He is in control of world events. It is clearly recorded for us within the sacred pages of Holy Writ that Jesus, the Messiah of God, will return. May we pour over the pages of Scripture and ponder and apply its truths.

If the religious Jewish scholars and religious Jewish people are anticipation the coming of Messiah and the Messianic Kingdom, how much more should evangelicals, who know theses truths and who know who the Messiah is, be anticipating His return? May we look up, for *our redemption draweth nigh!*

Perhaps Today!

Notes

1. Kushner, *"When Bad Things Happen to Good People,"* G.K. Hall & Co., Boston, Massachusetts, 1982, p. 82

2. Kac, "The Messiahship of Jesus," Baker Book House, Grand Rapids, Michigan, 1986, p. 36

3. Ibid., pp. 42,43

10

Dwelling in the New Jerusalem, New Heaven and Earth

The name *"New Jerusalem"* is found twice in Scripture. (Rev. 3:12; 21:2) It is believed that the New Jerusalem will be inhabited by the Church. John was told that he would be shown the bride, the Lamb's wife in Revelation 21:9, and he was shown the city, the New Jerusalem in 21:10,11. This city was not only given a name, the New Jerusalem, it also has walls, gates that are guarded by angels and only the redeemed can enter; its foundation is made of precious stones & jewels; it has citizens who are saved; it is 1500 miles square; it's glory is profound.

"Let not your heart be troubled: ye believe in God, believe also in me. In my Father's house are many mansions: if it were not so, I would have told you. I go to prepare a place for you. And if I go and prepare a place for you, I will come again, and receive you unto myself; that where I am, there ye may be also." John 14:1-3

However, some also believe that the inhabitants will include the Old Testament Saints according to Hebrews 11:8-16:

"By faith Abraham when he was called to go out to the place... obeyed...For he looked for a city which hath foundations, whose builder and maker is God...These all died in faith, not having received the promises, but having seen them afar off, and were persuaded of them, and embraced them, and confessed that they were strangers and pilgrims

*on the earth...Wherefore God is not ashamed to be called their God: for
He hath prepared for them a city."*

Nevertheless, the New Heaven and New Earth are a reference to a
perfected state of the universe and final dwelling of the righteous.

The idea of a New Heaven and New Earth runs deep in the vein of the
Jewish soul. Since the "Fall" of man in Genesis chapter three the
anticipation of Messiah coming and putting things in proper order is
woven throughout the fabric of Old Testament thought.

God promised Abraham's seed that they would inherit the land for a
"thousand generations." If a generation is 30 years, we are speaking
about 30,000 years. This will not happen unless there is a New Earth for
them to dwell. (Deut. 7:9; 1 Chron. 16:15; Psalm 105:8; Isa. 65:17;
66:22) Therefore, it is believed that the New Earth will be for Israel.

However, it is written, *"Eye hath not seen, nor ear heard, neither
have entered into the heart of man, the things which God hath prepared
for them that love him. But God hath revealed them unto us by his Spirit:
for the Spirit searcheth all things, yea, the deep things of God." (1 Cor.
2:9-10)* Though the New Jerusalem may be for the Church and the New
Earth for Israel, we will inhabit, rule with and participate in all that God
has for us. James states that we are *"a kind of first fruits of His crea-
tures."* (Jas. 1:18) If we are the *"first fruits"* then what must the whole
harvest be like?

We read, *"of the increase of His government and peace there shall
be no end."* (Isa. 9:7) This means that His government is limitless. Paul
said it this way, *"And when all things shall be subdued unto him, then
shall the Son also himself be subject unto him (God) that put all things
under him, that God may be all in all." (1 Cor. 15:28)* God is all in all,
just as Jesus is "all in all" (Col. 3:11) for they are equal.

The idea is that God has a plan so vast, so beyond anything we could
ever imagine, that one day all the universe with its galaxies, solar
systems, planets, stars, all that is realized and unrealized will yield to the
authority of Christ and the redeemed. This is known as the *Great
Abdication.*

Paul said in Romans 8:19,21, *"For the earnest expectation of the
creature waiteth for the manifestation of the sons of God...Because the
creature itself also shall be delivered from the bondage of corruption into*

the glorious liberty of the children of God." The curse will be removed and creation will be delivered. This will take place in two stages. The *first* stage will be during the Millennial Reign of Christ and the *second* stage with the New Heaven, New Earth & New Jerusalem.

Oh, what a glorious day that will be when all of creation will finally be brought into harmony with Messiah Jesus, when time as we know it will end and eternity begins. The "age to come" has no end and those who believe in Jesus will be there.

11

Shavuot: **Feast of Pentecost**

S havuot, or the Feast of Pentecost, is one of the seven feasts described in Leviticus 23. Originally, Shavuot was an agricultural feast. Eventually, it became known as the day Moses received the Law from Mt. Sinai

Historically, the Jews would celebrate Shavuot by reading the Books of Exodus focusing on the record of Moses receiving the Law. Also, the Book of Ruth would be read because of her devotion to the Law of God. Today, this tradition is still in vogue. Plus, thousands in Jerusalem, after studying the Scriptures all night, will trek to the Western Wall, and as the sun rises recite a morning liturgical prayer.

Shavuot is celebrated in late May or early June 50 days after Passover. Historically during the Passover, after the sacrificing of the lamb, 600,000 men (Exodus 12:37-38), approximately 3,000,000 Israelites total, left Egypt after being slaves for 400 years. Now *they are set free!*

What an awesome sight after they left Egypt for the Israelites to behold God's power at the Red Sea, then to receive manna from Heaven and water from the rock. Now, standing at the foot of a quaking Mt. Sinai in the desert they observe Moses, their leader and deliverer, ascend up into the very presence of God. It had been almost 2,000 years, since the time of Adam, that God displayed such communication to a man. Now, Moses is prostrate in His presence and the Jews are terrified.

Moses was gone for 40 days on the quaking mountain. The people became impatient and disobedient to God and had made and erected a Golden Calf. The Israelites began to worship this image of gold and as a punishment for their sin, 3,000 died by the sword of the Levites (Exodus 32:28).

Fifteen hundred years after the Exodus, following the sacrifice of Jesus (Yeshua) our "Passover Lamb" on Calvary, the Church was born. During Shavuot (Pentecost) the disciples, being in the upper room, were filled with the Holy Spirit. Peter began to preach which resulted in 3,000 souls being saved (Acts 2:41).

Look at the contrast! When the Law was given, 3,000 died. When the birthday of the Church unfolded, 3,000 received "Life." Paul stated, *"the law was our schoolmaster to bring us unto Christ (Messiah)"* (Galatians 3:24). The Law, therefore, being holy (Romans 7:12) points us to someone greater than itself, namely Messiah. The Law is holy and we would not have known about sin except through the Law (Romans 7:7,12). *"But where sin abounded, grace did much more abound"* (Romans 5:20).

Grace reigns in Jesus our Messiah. Life, peace and purpose are found in Him. Therefore, Shavuot, or the Feast of Pentecost directs us to a truth greater than the Law. It is through the Lord Jesus and His shed blood that anyone, who trusts in Him, will be *set free* from the condemnation of the Law. Eternal life is the gift for those who believe. This is the message Peter preached on Shavuot, as he proclaimed Jesus to be both "Lord and Messiah" by virtue of the resurrection (Acts 2:14-36).

"For the law was given by Moses, but grace and truth came by Jesus Christ." (John 1:17)

This is the message of the Church that was birthed on the day of Shavuot. The Church is the mystery that was originally hidden, but now revealed. (Ephesians 3) The Church is the representation of the Lord Jesus on earth. Therefore, let the Church manifest grace and truth. May the Church reflect Jesus!

12

Why Jerusalem?

The fuse that ignited the recent wave of violence in the Middle East was when Ariel Sharon visited the Temple Mount in the year 2000. This site is known to Muslims as Haram al-Sharif or the Noble Sanctuary. To Jews and Christians it is known as the Temple Mount.

Why all the fuss over Israel? Why all the tension over the Holy City Jerusalem? Why is the Temple Mount so important?

In the next moments we will discuss some of the key factors that make Jerusalem the most important city in the world.

The Temple Mount in the heart of Jerusalem is where the Jewish Temple stood in Biblical times. The Western or "Wailing" Wall is a retaining wall located on the western side of where the Temple stood, thus making this the most important religious site to religious Jews.

Religious Jews believe that the Temple Mount is where redemption will take place when the Messiah comes. Christians also recognize this location is where the prophets and angels said Jesus would return. To give up this holy site, to give up on the city itself is like giving up on the hope for redemption. If the Messiah is to come to Jerusalem, then you hold on to this most important piece of real estate.

For the Muslims, the Haram al-Sharif is where the Dome of the Rock is located and the al-Aqsa Mosque, Islam's third holiest site. They believe this is the place where the Prophet Mohammed ascended to heaven.

In the 1967 war Israel captured the Western Wall. In fact the whole of Jerusalem is now under Israeli control except the Temple Mount where Muslims oversee the area. The Palestinians are desirous to have their capital in East Jerusalem. This is a vital factor for any future Palestinian State.

There has been a lot of political jockeying regarding how to solve this problem regarding Jerusalem. Some suggestions have been from full Israeli sovereignty to twin capitals to sharing government control over the city.

So why Jerusalem?

The current Middle East Crisis is not a surprise to the student of the bible. Events unfolding are exactly how the prophets said they would happen. To understand what God is doing in the world we need to understand what God is doing with Israel. Specifically Jerusalem!

The History

- The first mention of Jerusalem is found in Genesis 14:8 where the city is called Salem. Salem means "peace."

- Ezekiel mentions that the area was once populated by the Amorites and Hittites (Ezekiel 16:3).

- Jerusalem is also in the area of Moriah where Abraham bound Isaac (Genesis 22).

- God gave to David the city, via conquest, from the Jebusites around 1,004 BC, over thee thousand years ago (1 Chronicles 11:4-9).

- David bought a threshing floor for 50 shekels of silver (2 Samuel 24:24) and built an altar unto the Lord. (same area where Abraham bound Isaac).

- This threshing floor is where Solomon, David's son, built the Temple (2 Chronicles 3:1).

- This is the site of the second temple and the temple that Herod embellished in the time of Jesus.

- Jesus rode into the city as people praised and worshiped Him as Messiah.

- Jesus was crucified outside Jerusalem's walls.

- Jesus ascended to the Father from the Mount of Olives overlooking the Temple.

The Future

- Jerusalem will be the sight of the Tribulation Temple (2 Thessalonians 2:1-4).

- Jerusalem will be hated by all nations (Zechariah 12:2,3).

- Jerusalem will be surrounded by armies (Zechariah 14:1,2).

- Messiah will descend in this area (Zechariah 14:3,4).

- This is where the Millennial Temple will stand (Ezekiel 40; Zechariah 2,3).

- God desires Jerusalem (Psalm 132:14).

- Jerusalem will be the center of Messiah's Kingdom.

- Jerusalem will be the global capital (Isaiah 2:2-4).

So now we can begin to understand why Jerusalem is so important to God's program and the people of the world.

In Zechariah 2:1-13 we find the 3rd of 8 visions. Verses 4 & 5 bring to light that there will be a noteworthy increase in the population of

Jerusalem in the latter days. The Scripture states that Jews will flock to
Jerusalem from the four corners of the earth.

Verse 8 reinforces the Abrahamic Covenant (*bless them that bless
thee and curse him that curseth thee*) inasmuch as those that touch Israel,
touches the *apple* or pupil, the most sensitive part of God's eye.

When David conquered the city, as directed by God in 1 Chronicles
chapter 11, Jerusalem became central in world events. Jewish sages call
Jerusalem *"the very center of the earth."* They also teach that, *"living in
the land of Israel equals the performance of all the commandments of the
Torah."*

Jerusalem has been called by more than 70 different names. For
example:

1. "Lion of God" (Isa. 29:1)
2. "Joy" (Isa. 65:18)
3. "City of Truth" (Zech. 8:3)
4. "Throne of God" (Jer. 3:17)

Very simply, God has chosen Jerusalem.

God says of Jerusalem, *"This is my rest for ever: here will I dwell;
for I desire it"* (Ps. 132:14). Also, *"Behold, I have graven thee upon the
palms of my hands; thy walls are continually before me"* (Isa. 49:16).

As Christians, everything we believe and hold dear comes from
Jerusalem. Jerusalem is truly "the joy of the whole earth." (Psalm 48:2)
From Jerusalem, we have the most important events of the Lord's life and
our redemption recorded for us. Plus, from Jerusalem the Gospel went
out to four corners of the earth (Acts 1:8).

Jerusalem is not only the key in world events of the past, but the
future as well. From Isaiah 2:2-4, we learn that Jerusalem will be the
geographical heart of the Millennial Kingdom of Messiah. Jerusalem will
be the central government for the world. How exciting this will be! How
glorious! However, between then and now, Jerusalem, though a joy to
Christians and to Jewish people, will become a burden to the world.
(Zechariah 12:2,3).

Joel 3:1,2 records for us that Jerusalem is God's place of Judgment
(Jehoshaphat means God judges). The Scripture warns us of a time that

is called *"the time of Jacob's trouble"*(Jer. 30:7). This is a time of terrible calamity concerning the Middle East, specifically Israel. You see there is something about Jerusalem that causes the world to fear and marvel. (Psalm 48:1-6)

Why?

Some 2600 years ago, the world had an immeasurable paradigm shift as it entered into what is called the Gentile Age. This happened when the governmental structure of Israel was ended by the Babylonians in 586 B.C. The sovereign State of Israel would not be restored until the 20th century. Daniel saw this paradigm shift in a vision, as an image of a man. (Dan. 2:31-45)

He saw:

1. Head of Gold—Nebuchadnezzar and his Babylonian Kingdom (606—538 B.C.)
2. Chest & Arms of Silver—Media-Persia (538-333 B.C.)
3. Belly & Thighs of Bronze—Greece (333-63 B.C.)
4. Legs of Iron with feet and toes of iron and clay—Rome

Daniel records that these empires end suddenly because of a stone that crashes into the image. Who is the stone? It is the Messiah!

Jesus who was crucified and rose again in Jerusalem, the Son of the Living God, the Rose of Sharon, the Root of Jesse, the Lion of Judah who crushes the Kingdoms of the world (Dan. 2:34,44).

Meanwhile, the rising of Israel this century and particularly Jerusalem being once again under Jewish control (1967, Six-day War) poses quite a problem for the world. As Malcom Hedding writes,

> *The rise of Jerusalem not only threatens all governments…it is a grave threat to all false philosophies. The rise of Jerusalem shatters the…myth God is dead (or not involved in human events)…the reestablishment of Jerusalem …(is) the work of a living God. The rise of Jerusalem challenges all false theologies such as Christian Anti-Semitism, Dominion or Replacement*

Theology. The rise of Jerusalem is also a threat to philosophies and theologies of lawlessness, for in a resurrected Jerusalem, we simply must face the ideas of God's law and God's judgment. We can begin to understand the reason for the rage and madness which Jerusalem incites throughout the whole earth.
In short...Israel is a foreign body, she is unwanted in our world."

— Malcom Hedding, "Understanding Israel,"
published by Zion's Gate Publishing

This hatred will begin to culminate when a massive coalition bent on the destruction of Israel, recorded for us in Ezekiel 38 & 39, launches a sophisticated attack against Israel during the first part of the Tribulation (Time of Jacob's Trouble). *Fortunately*, God intervenes and the coalition is defeated. *Unfortunately*, the Anti-Christ will come into full power and set himself up as Messiah. While in Jerusalem, inside the rebuilt Temple, the False Prophet will set up an image of the Beast. Daniel called this, *"the abomination of desolation"* (11:31) in which the Beast, his image and Satan himself, will be worshipped. (Rev. 13:4,15)

Those who do not worship the Beast or his image will be killed. This will be a time of persecution such as the world has never known before. The persecution will be primarily targeted against the Jew, but embracing all people who do not worship the Beast or dissent from the policies of the Beast.

A new economic world system will be announced. All people on the planet will be required to receive a mark, the *mark of the beast* imprinted on their flesh. Without this mark one cannot buy, or sell or transact any business. To reject this system or befriend a Jew or believe on the Lord Jesus could be fatal. The Great Terror foretold will have come.

The World will eventually become disillusioned with the Anti-Christ as he will be unable to solve the global problems that will unfold according to the book of Revelation.

As a result the kings of the East will begin to move against him. The final and worst series of battles will begin to unfold. Armageddon will begin (Rev. 16:12-21). The horrors and dread of this campaign are beyond anything history has recorded.

Just when the madness and hellish carnage brought about by these armies seem endless. Just when all hope is gone and these forces seem undefeatable, Jesus, the Messiah, the glory of Israel and the light of the Gentiles, personally and visibly returns to the Mount of Olives splitting the mountain in two. (Zechariah 14:1-4) The Millennial Kingdom will begin, the Messianic age of peace will have begun, *"Thy Kingdom come, Thy will be done."*

What a story! What a glorious beginning for Jerusalem, then a very bumpy journey, and finally, peace and prosperity. These events are true as they are written within the pages of Scripture. I did not give you all the details, as time and space would not allow. However, you have a brief synopsis of what will be taking place and why all the fuss about Jerusalem. The world marvels at this glorious city. It is the key to understanding what God is doing in this world and His blueprint for the world.

We are given a mandate from God in Psalm 122:6 to *"Pray for the peace of Jerusalem."* There will be *no* peace *until* the "Prince of Peace" comes. Therefore, we are praying for the Lord's return when we pray for the peace of Jerusalem, *"Thy kingdom come, Thy will be done."* Also, we are praying for the *"remnant"* that will be saved during this time of the age of the Church (Romans 11:5).

May those who believe in Jesus stand with Israel and bless her through the hard times and the good times. All prophecy centers on God's ancient people, the promised land of Israel, the golden City of Jerusalem and the God of Abraham.

God is moving in the events of Israel and specifically Jerusalem. Jesus said,

"And when these things begin to come to pass, then look up, and lift up your heads; for your redemption draweth nigh." (Lk. 21:28-31)

13

A Report on Israel—2002

*The soldier turned his back and as I
moved the barbed wire…*

Upon arriving in Israel it was very noticeable the changes that had taken place the last two years and since September 11. Security was intense, police and soldiers were everywhere. In fact, before boarding El Al in Zurich I, along with others, was thoroughly interrogated, my bags were opened and searched, my shoes and clothing were checked and I was frisked. Security was tight. There was a definite tension in the air.

After landing in Israel my contact picked me up and took me to the apartment where I would be staying. The apartment was located in the midst of an orthodox community within Jerusalem. From my veranda I was able to see the Knesset.

The next several days I began to meet with my appointments. The main purpose of my trek to Israel was to answer the question, "How can I, as an itinerant bible teacher, and how can Israel Today Ministries help in the humanitarian efforts in the Middle East?"

At first I was with the director of Tantur Institute in Gilo, located in the Southern part of Jerusalem that sits atop a hill overlooking Beit Jala & bordering Bethlehem in the West Bank. The stonewalls of the institution border the road leading into Bethlehem.

Within the walls of this massive institution there were a myriad of people who were unable to return to their homes because of the curfew set by Israel upon the West Bank. The people inside the institute, mostly Palestinian, were serving food, maintenance and other tasks for their room and board until the curfew was lifted.

From the top of the roof of the Tantur I saw across the valley into Bethlehem. There we saw plumes of dust created by the tanks and armored vehicles as they tracked through the streets of the city. I saw people trying to be stealth as they were going from one place to another. It was a vivid reminder of the signs of the times in which we live.

My next appointment was with the president of the Bethlehem Bible College. Because of the curfew I was unable to meet with him. However, I was able to meet with one of the professors.

We were able to talk for several hours. I shared with him that I came to Israel, as "a learner" and that I wanted to understand the plight of the Palestinian Christian and the Palestinian community in general. He was pleased that I came to learn and not to come with "all the answers as so many Americans do."

Arrangements were made to "sneak" me in the back way into Bethlehem the next day if the curfew was still in place. Fortunately, the curfew was lifted for six hours and we were able to drive through the checkpoint pass the soldiers, tanks and armored vehicles into the city.

People by the hundreds were out in the streets procuring needed food and other necessities. Bethlehem Bible College had postponed their graduation because of the trouble between Israel and terrorists. Now they had a window to proceed. It was amazing! There were only six hours to obtain needed foodstuff and yet the Christians spent three of those six in the college chapel to hear the preaching of the gospel and to honor the graduates.

Brother Andrew, "God's Smuggler", was the guest speaker. At seventy-four years of age, he is still traveling to hot spots around the world bringing bibles to those in need.

We were able to meet several Christian families; also, the governor of Bethlehem was in attendance. There was much joy and celebration over the young men and women graduating. Some were going to start churches and others were going to teach and work with children.

Soon, the curfew was once again engaged. Therefore, I and a host of others had to quickly leave. Streets were being closed. Hundreds of people were trying to leave Bethlehem. Tanks and armored vehicles began to move.

We found ourselves in a situation where we would not be able to leave. The road we were traveling was closed. We dropped off all the passengers at one point. Then we approached a soldier and asked if we could cross. Barbed wire was across the road. We must leave, but the road is closed. If you are out in the street after curfew you could be arrested.

The soldier willingly turned his back, and as I moved the barbed wire we drove the van through. I then moved the wire back and we thanked the soldier for his kindness. After driving through the check point we were able to pick up those we dropped off on the other side of the point.

A few days later I was able to worship with these Palestinian Christians. The Baptist church worshipped with the Nazarene church as their building was in repair. They sang for an hour, preached for an hour and fellowshipped and ate together for a few hours more. The Christian community is very small in Israel. The concept of Christian community and that of needing each other is very real. They depend on each other. They pray for each other. There is no time for fussing about silly things that American Christians complain about (i.e. too hot; too cold; too long; too short; too deep; too light; too loud; too soft et al). They simply wanted to be together and worship the Lord Jesus!

At the conclusion of my time with the Palestinian Christians they thanked me for my humble spirit and willingness to understand. They offered to be a blessing and to assist me and the ministry of Israel Today Ministries' humanitarian outreach. We now have an open door within the Palestinian Christian community in Israel.

It was only a few days later when terrorists stopped a bus of Israelis going home and opened fire upon them. Many were killed. Even as women and children were crawling out of the bus to escape, they were shot to death. Then a couple of day's later suicide bombers killed more people in Tel Aviv. This was vivid reminder why Israel enforces curfew upon these areas that house and train terrorists.

There are innocent victims on both sides of this issue. The Christian community, both Palestinian and Messianic are suffering and experiencing persecution and rejection.

I then had opportunity to meet with two Messianic community organizations and individuals who have a desire to reach people with the gospel and humanitarian aid.

I was introduced to a team of believers who move food and clothing in bulk to those in need. There are literally thousands of families in Israel waiting for help. There are boys and girls who do not have basic food necessities. There are mothers and fathers wanting to meet the needs of their family. They only need a little help to stand on their feet.

Beloved, I came home with my eyes wide open. Over one in four Israelis is living in poverty. Approximately one of every two Palestinians is impoverished. There are victims on both sides of the issue.

Together as evangelicals we can bring food and clothing to these families in need. Together, we can bring a cup of milk in the name of Jesus to a family; a piece of bread to feed the old; a blanket to bring warmth to a mother in the cool of the night; we can bring the gospel of peace through Jesus the Messiah to those who do not know Him.

Our time in Israel has provided more open doors. I.T.M now has the means to bring the gospel and humanitarian aid into the Middle East.

With your prayers, support and involvement we can bless Israel and make a difference in these last days before Jesus returns.

"Inasmuch as ye have done it unto one of the least of these my brethren, ye have done it unto me."—Jesus, Matthew 25:40

14

The Hem of His Garment

And behold a woman…touched the
hem of his garment.

— *Matthew 9:20*

This moving story of the woman touching the hem of the Lord's garment can also be found in Mark 5:28 & Luke 8:44. Why did she want to touch Him? Why does the emphasis seem to focus upon the *"hem"* of Christ's robe?

The hem is called a *"Tzitzit"* in Hebrew. God commanded that these fringes on the corners of their garments be worn in obedience to Him (Numbers 15:37-40). The tzitzit was to remind the Jews of all the commandments of the Lord. Jesus, being an observant Jew would have worn them on the outside of his "over-garment." This would have been like a heavy outer garment worn today by many Bedouins. The tzitzit was not merely a fringe decoration; rather it was the most holy part of the garment.

Why would the woman be desirous to touch the hem or tzitzit of the Lord's outer garment? The prophet Malachi stated that, *"the Sun of righteousness [will] arise with healing in His wings" (Malachi 4:3)*. You see, the tzitzit (plural *tzitziyot*) were also referred to as "Wings." The woman obviously understood the prophecy and knew that if she could only touch the "Wings" of his garment she could be healed. This garment would also have been the Lord's *"prayer shawl"* as well as a garment to keep warm at night and to keep the sun off by day.

Notice that she, being defiled by this disease, after touching the Holy, was made whole. Understand, that the prophet Haggai (2:11-13) made it very clear that if the unclean touches the clean, the clean shall become unclean. They feared that if the unholy would touch the holy, the holy would become defiled.

Oh, beloved, **NOT SO WITH JESUS!** A few verses later He even touched the dead body of the ruler's daughter and she rose from the dead. It was against the tradition of Judaism to touch the unclean, and yet, the Lord took the dead girl's hand, "and she arose."

The Lord does the impossible. He is the God of miracles. At times, He breaks all the tradition of men, for His ways are not our ways. He takes the unclean and makes them clean. He forgives our sins and casts them into the depths of the sea and remembers them no more. He spoke the worlds into existence. He walked on water and fed the multitudes. He rose from the dead and is coming again.

Jesus said, *"Inasmuch as ye have done it unto one of the least of these my brethren, ye have done it unto me (Matthew 25:40)"*

Lord, help me show Israel the "hem of [Your] garment" so they may touch [You] and be made whole.

15

Blessing

I will bless them that bless thee….

— *Genesis* 12:3

J ewish life is replete with "berakhot"—blessings. Blessings for food & wine. Blessings for smelling fragrant oils, fruits & plants. Blessings for sight & hearing and so forth.

Perhaps the most intriguing blessing is the "Birkat Kohanim", or the "Priestly Blessing" sometimes called "Aarons' Blessing."

"The Lord bless thee, and keep thee: The Lord make his face shine upon thee, and be gracious unto thee: The Lord lift up his countenance upon thee, and give thee peace." Numbers 6:24-26

The blessing was recited daily by the priests. They would ascend to a special platform, cover their heads and with outstretched arms recited the ancient blessing.

The blessing starts with petition for material blessing, then spiritual blessing and finally the greatest blessing of all "Shalom"—Peace.

The blessing points the pilgrim to a personal encounter with God. This is the only way to find true peace. The Lord Jesus became the "Passover Lamb", the atonement for sin. The prophet stated that the Messiah *"was wounded for our transgressions, he was bruised for our iniquities: the chastisement of our peace was upon him; and with his stripes we are healed."* Isaiah 53:5

As a result of the cross, you and I can have a personal encounter with God through the shed blood of the Messiah, the Lord Jesus, by trusting in Him alone for salvation.

Jesus said He was the Messiah and His life, death and resurrection was proof. It is only through the Messiah, the Lord Jesus that you and I can fully understand and experience Aaron's Blessing in finding true provision, purpose and peace.

16

Life

I am come that they might have life.

— *John* 10:10

Beloved,
We have been given a great gift, namely the gift of life! *"And the Lord God formed man of the dust of the ground, and breathed into his nostrils the breath of life; and man became a living soul" (Genesis 2:7).* By virtue of this act man has been given a special relationship with his creator. For *"man alone has the breath of life blown into his nostrils by God Himself. Only by virtue of this direct animation did man become a living being, drawing directly from God his life source."*[1] Paul stated on Mars Hill in Athens before the philosophers that God *"giveth to all life, and breath...for in him we live, and move and have our being" (Acts 17:25,28).*

We are different from the beasts of the field in that beasts react instinctively while humans express *"intellect, free will, self-awareness, consciousness of the existence of others, conscience, responsibility and self control."*[2] Therefore, human life is precious and has purpose. David writes, *"For I am fearfully and wonderfully made...how precious also are thy thoughts unto me" (Psalm 139:14,17).* Beloved, remember, *you* are here this hour, this minute, this second, in this universe, on this planet for a reason. You are no mistake—God makes no mistakes.

One scholar makes this observation of the Hebrew word *"life"* (HaYYiM or HYYM, no vowels in Hebrew, simply vowel sounds). *"The word for life in Hebrew ends with (YiM), the grammatical indicator of plurality. We are granted not one life, but two."*[3]

Indeed, this scholar is correct in his statement, as truly we *"are granted"* two lives. One life is spent here on earth, and the other will be spent in eternity. In terms of eternity, the Scripture speaks of two eternal places of existence, namely, Heaven or Hell. This Jewish scholar continues his statement by saying, *"Central to the word 'HaYYiM' (the Hebrew word for life), are two YY's (two 'yuds', the smallest of Hebrew letters) which, combined, form the name of God."*[4]

Now here is an interesting thought! Central to the Hebrew word for life is the name of God. The Apostle John tells us that Jesus is the very essence of *"life"* (John 1:3,4). Jesus is God, and those who trust in Him alone as Savior and Messiah will spend eternity in the presence of God, who is central to all life. Jesus said, *"I am the way, the truth, and the life: no man cometh unto the Father, but by me" (John 14:6)*. John also stated, *"He that believeth on the Son hath everlasting life: and he that believeth not the Son shall not see life: but the wrath of God abideth on Him" (John 3:36)*.

Jesus also declares, *" But he that believeth not is condemned already" (John 3:18)*. This condemnation and wrath is a reference to Hell. Those who have not believed that Jesus is the Messiah will spend their eternal existence in a Godless Hell full of pain and misery forever. (Luke 16; Revelation 20) Those who put their trust and faith in Jesus for salvation will spend eternal with God in Heaven.

Though found in Jewish literature and taught in rabbinical circles, that God is central to life, many Jewish people are unaware that Jesus is God and Messiah. These precious souls are so close and yet so far from the truth concerning Jesus (Hebrew: *Yeshua*).

O beloved, how this breaks my heart! Will you help God's ancient people find true *"Life"* in Messiah Jesus?

Notes

1. Nahum M. Sarna, "Understanding Genesis, The Heritage of Biblical Israel," (Schocken Books, New York, 1970), p. 14

2 Ibid., p. 16

3. Benjamin Blech, "the Secrets of Hebrew Words," (Jason Aronson, Inc., New Jersey, 1991), p. 45

4. Ibid., p. 47

17

Israel 2003

All I want to do is to save some money and marry
my girl friend. I hope for peace. It is bad right
now. I must stay and help my country. They kill
babies and women. I must stay and help.

I have been to Israel several times and to walk where Jesus walked and
to see the beloved city of David, Jerusalem the golden, is always an
emotional experience. When you walk the rugged stony highways and
byways the bible comes alive for you, plus, you feel the tension of the
people as they wait for the attack from the terrorist or from an evil
dictator in some rouge country.

When you are in Israel you find your heart belongs there. You begin
to understand the history and the biblical significance of *eretz Yisrael*, the
land of Israel. As one Jewish shop keeper said, *"When your feet step on
the plane and you go back to America, you'll discover that part of your
heart is left here in Israel."* He is right!

The prophet said that Israel will *blossom like a rose*. Indeed, as you
look upon the hills you see green, flowers and multitudinous trees. Life
is pulsating with messianic hope. The religious Jew is faithfully and
passionately praying for peace. With every ounce of strength and hope the
secular Jew wants to live a normal life without the threat of terrorism.

"All I want to do is to save some money and marry my girl friend. I hope for peace. It is bad right now. I must stay and help my country. They kill babies and women. I must stay and help."

These are the words of Samuel, a 24 year-old taxi driver in Jerusalem. He was stationed in Jenin after all the trouble started when terrorists, once again, attacked Israel. All this young man wants to do is to live in peace and to raise a family.

A few days later while traveling throughout Jerusalem with Dr. John Baird, one of our board members who accompanied me, a man dressed in Intifata (uprising) garb tried to run us off the road. Our Jewish driver was calm as he swerved out of the way of this madman who was bent on harming us. Our driver simply stated, *"Intifata, crazy!"*

Children playing in the streets, mothers caring for their babies, fathers watching constantly surveying the crowd for any potential danger, and young people starting out in life and falling in love, trying to make ends meet. This is what you find in Israel. Yet, the news media paints a picture that is quite different. They portray Israel as the one who is occupying and like Goliath attempting to intimidate the little guy. However, the truth is that Israelis simply want to live in peace without bloodshed.

Remember, every time an Israeli steps foot on a bus, or walks down the street or goes shopping a terrorist may be waiting around the corner plotting a dastardly deed. A few months ago in a religious school, terrorists opened fire and killed several students while they were eating in the cafeteria. While I was in the Ben Yehuda area, an area with shops, stores, restaurants, a bomb scare unfolded. Police blocked streets and kept the people away as they checked out a suspicious package. Fortunately, it was a false alarm. Also, while I was in Israel, at a bus station in Tel Aviv, two suicide bombers detonated their explosives killing and injuring multitudes. Tell me, who is the victim? The terrorist? The suicide bomber? NO! A RESOUNDING NO! *Israel is the victim!*

In this land of contrast we also find the innocent, those who are hungry and in need, having no shelter, clothing and other basic necessities. *Along with the preaching and the teaching of the Word of God* I am committed to help with the humanitarian relief needed in Israel.

Those of us that have been the recipient of the grace of God through Jesus the Messiah owe a debt to the Jew. It was the Jewish disciples of

Jesus who first brought the gospel of grace to the Gentile. Therefore the Apostle Paul wrote in Romans 15:27 that *the Gentile is a debtor to the Jew for the spiritual things they received.* Paul furthermore emphasizes that it is the duty of the Gentile believer to *help in the Jews material needs.*

Israel Today Ministries is committed to:

1. Teach the church about Israel *(through sound bible teaching)*

2. Teach Israel about their Messiah *(through acts of charity and presenting the gospel)*

3. Help feed & clothe those in need *(to fulfill the mandate of Romans 15:17 & Genesis 12:1-3)*

   Time is short, life is precious and Jesus is coming soon!

18

Isaac Was Comforted

And Isaac brought her into his mother Sarah's tent, and took Rebekah, and she became his wife; and he loved her: and Isaac was comforted after his mother's death.

— *Genesis* 24:67

This is a peculiar verse. What does it mean *"Isaac was comforted after his mother's death"*? What void did Rebekah fill? What was so significant in this event that caused the Holy Spirit to guide Moses to record this vignette of Isaac's life?

To understand this verse is to understand the role of the woman in Jewish culture. God said concerning Adam, *"It is not good that the man should be alone: I will make him an help meet for him" (Genesis 2:18)*. The emphasis here is that *"It is NOT good"* this lonesomeness of man. Therefore, *"I will make him an help meet"* meaning, 'one who rescues'.

The woman plays a most important role in the Jewish home especially regarding the Sabbath day observance. Sabbath or Shabbat is the holiest day of the week. It is the time between the sun setting on Friday evening and the sun setting on Saturday evening. It is a time of worship, scripture reading, prayer, a special meal, special bread, lighting of candles, rest, remembering the Creator and His creation, and a celebration of life. *"Remember the Sabbath day, to keep it holy" (Exodus 20:8).*

Sarah, Isaac's mother, had passed away and left a huge void in the life of the family. When she was alive her presence nurtured a reminder of the blessings of God. As the *one who rescues* she would light the candles each Shabbat. She would prepare the Challah dough, the rising dough, the "miraculous increase" of the special bread. From the lit candles, which are symbols of hope, from the light she created, a cloud would form that hovered in, throughout and over the tent. Passersby would notice the hazy cloud. The delicate scent of the candle would kiss the senses of anyone near its glow. The tent itself was an insignia of provision and safety.

Understanding these truths we are reminded that the weekly tasks Sarah performed were wonderfully symbolic. They pointed to the great hope that one day Messiah will come and bring redemption. That messianic anticipation pulsated within the veins of Jewish belief. This profound hope is pronounced clearly within the Scriptures.

The Light

The light of the candle represents the light of God. When the Menorah, (the seven branch candle in the Temple) was lit, it is said, the light emanating from its golden lamp dispelled the darkness and shadows from all the corners of the Temple, and from there, throughout the whole world. Sarah's act of lighting the candles leads us to the truth that the Light of God's love dispels the darkness of sin and brings hope to the recipient. Jesus said it this way, *"I am the light of the world: he that followeth me shall not walk in darkness, but shall have the light of life" (John 8:12).*

Jesus, the Messiah, shed His blood on cruel Roman cross. He became our sin offering, our Passover lamb, so that anyone, who believes in Him, will be redeemed receiving eternal life. Without the shedding of blood there is no forgiveness of sin (Hebrews 9:22).

The Light within Sarah's tent is a type of Jesus the Messiah who IS the Light that dispels the darkness of sin in the heart of man. For those who receive Jesus as Savior will experience, hope, life, joy, forgiveness and light (John 1:1-17).

The Bread

The *Challah* bread reminds us of the provision of God. *"Give us this day our daily bread."* Bread and water are the main staples in the wilderness. Christians are pilgrims just passing through the wilderness of this life.

Our lives speak volumes as to who we are. We belong to the Most High God. We are in this world, however, we are not of the world. We live, work and interact within the construct of this world and its social system. Christians are salt and light in their community. Believers must embrace life with a passion, as life is a gift from God. We must never be hesitant to experience the fullness of humanity as we are created in God's image. Therefore, as Christians, we must move forward in our journey knowing that the Lord is with us and that He will never leave us without provision.

Every morning the Israelites found manna from God, the bread from heaven. Likewise, we must daily make the journey and search for those delightful treasures God has provided tailored just for us. You will discover hope, joy, peace, goodness, compassion and mercy to name a few blessings of God's provision.

God's grace is always evident throughout our "pilgrim's progress." Even when we walk through the valleys of testing, trial and sorrow, we find wonderful treasures. We discover the golden nuggets of God's provision, the sweet smell and taste of the warm and, miraculously increasing, never-ending *bread* of God's grace and mercy.

The *Challah* (twisted bread) that Sarah baked was symbolic of God's watchful provision in the wilderness. It is a common bread like the bread at Pentecost (Hebrew—*Shavuot*). All are welcome. As she kneaded the dough we are reminded of that we are clay in the Master's hand. The sweet smell of rising dough causes us to remember that Jesus has given himself for us as a sweet fragrant offering and sacrifice to God (Ephesians 5:2).

When Abraham and Isaac entered the tent where Sarah was baking the bread they were brought face to face with the hope of the Messiah, the Anointed One, the Bread of Life. One day He will come. In fact, He did!

Jesus, our Lord and Savior, is our "Bread." He is the "Bread of Life." He is our sustenance. Without Him we can do nothing (John 15:5). He is the living Word, therefore, we are sustained by learning from Him (Matthew 11:29; John 1:1,14).

We learn from Him by reading the Scriptures. Jesus said, *"I am the bread of life: he that cometh to me shall never hunger; and he that believeth on me shall never thirst"* (John 6:35).

Sarah was doing more that just baking bread. She was showing us *"The Way, The Truth and The Life"* (John 14:6).

The Cloud

The cloud from the candle that hovered in, throughout and above the tent reminds us of God's presence. The cloud is symbolic of the Shechinah glory that was present in the wilderness in the form of a cloud. It was also present in the Tabernacle and Temple. The cloud also appeared on the Mount of Transfiguration. It represents God's Glory.

The presence of the cloud reminded those near its splendor, awe and terror that God is Holy and to be reverenced. People knew that God was worshipped and was present when they walked by Sarah's tent. There is something different about people when they worship God. There is clear evidence that a person has placed their faith and trust in the Lord Jesus as they become a new creature (2 Corinthians 5:17). There is something unique and wonderful about those who believe in God. The glory that Jesus had with the Father, *before the world was,* He has given to those who believe in Him (John 17:5,22). It will be clear to all that you are a child of God. The glory of God will be upon you. Passersby will know you are a follower of God.

The Tent

When we think of the "tent" we think of the Tabernacle sometimes called the "tent of meeting" the place where the Israelites and all the people were called to meet God. The Tabernacle or Tent was patterned after the heavenly tabernacle (Hebrews 8:2; 9:11; Revelation 13:6; 15:5; 21:3). Subsequently we are reminded of the eternal where God dwells and where the saints abode. The Tent was a place of activity, responsibility and service.

The Tent was also symbolic of the relationship between husband and wife. God told Moses to have the men return to their tents, meaning go back to your wives (Deuteronomy 5:30; 20:7). Paul taught that the relationship between husband and wife represent the mystical, mysterious and miraculous union between the church and Messiah (Ephesians 5:22-33). Believers in Jesus are one with God. Jesus is God!

Rebekah

Rebekah (Hebrew—*Rivkah*) brought joy, brightness, hope, life and a renewed faith as the spirit of God dwelled in her. Isaac was comforted by her presence mentally, emotionally, physically and spiritually. This is true of anyone who believes in Messiah Jesus. Jesus said, *"I am come that they might have life, and that they might have it more abundantly"* (John 10:10).

The Lord brings peace, joy, life, fullness, purpose, provision, protection, and comfort. We are complete in Him (Colossians 2:10) and through Him we will find totality of life in the human experience and in the eternal hope.

Jesus said, *"Come unto me, all ye that labour and are heavy laden, and I will give you rest. Take my yoke upon you, and learn of me; for I am meek and lowly in heart: and ye shall find rest unto your souls. For my yoke is easy, and my burden is light"* (Matthew 11:28-30).

"Isaac was comforted."

19

The Wonder
of Babylon (Iraq)

O ur eyes were glued to the news channel as American tanks rolled into Baghdad. To see the statue come down and watch the people respond to the falling of a dictatorial regimen was nothing less than awesome.

This area of the world is replete with drama, mystery and intrigue. In fact, this geographical area generally known as Mesopotamia is where history began. It is a tale of two cities—Jerusalem the city of God & Babylon the city of man. It is a tale of Light verses Dark. It is a tale of Good verses Evil. Let's go back and review some of the highlights of this fascinating area of the world, and then, fast-forward to the end of days to see what God says about Babylon.

Tigris and Euphrates Rivers

Within sight of these two veins of precious life-giving water is where God magnificently created man. This was the original home of paradise, the Garden of Eden. The rivers embraced the Garden and nurtured its splendor (Genesis 2:10,14).

Somewhere near the rivers the episode of Adam and Eve took place, and where sin entered the world (Genesis 2,3). Here the saga of the first murder, the killing of Abel unfolded (Genesis 4). Here is where the Cherubim were assigned *"to keep the way of the tree of life"* (Genesis 3:24). Perhaps the earliest inhabitants of this region were the Sumerians. The Bible refers to them as the people of the *"land of Shinar"* (Genesis 10:10). Many scholars believe that *Sargon*, who united the cities of Shinar (c. 3000 - 2300 B.C.), is none other than Nimrod (Genesis 10:8). If the rivers could only speak, the stories they could tell.

Nimrod

In Genesis 10 we read of Nimrod, the grandson of Ham through Cush, who was a mighty tyrant in the sight of God. He was, if you will, the first dictator. The text reads, *"He was a mighty hunter"* (vs. 9), emphasizing that he hunted men, rather than animals.

"And the beginning of his kingdom was Babel" (vs. 10). Nimrod is the founder of the Babylonian empire and was behind the building of a sophisticated tower that unified the world with one purpose. The purpose was to be greatly known and powerful. The city symbolized "political, social, and military unity", whereas, the tower symbolized "religious, economic and scientific unity." This tower originally was an observatory for astronomical studies. It was a Ziggurat whose top was not to literally "reach" heaven; rather, it was topped with a cultic temple to the stars. This man-made mountain started out as a scientific structure associated with astronomy and then became a source of pride and religious expression (Genesis 11).

The Rebellion

God commissioned Noah to have man scatter throughout and repopulate the world. The descendants of Noah failed to carry out this mandate from the Lord. Nimrod purposely rebelled against the Lord's instruction. Becoming defiant he endeavored to unify the people of the world. (This is exactly what the Anti-Christ will try to do). As a result of this rebellion God scattered the peoples of the earth so that His mandate could be fulfilled. Ultimately, God's purpose on earth will be done in spite of man's rebellion.

Josephus implies that Nimrod, this hunter of men and rebel against God, is the "father of heathenism" (Antiquities of the Jews, Book 1, chapter 4:2-3). He was the first ruler, the first dictator establishing a significant empire, and in fact founding several empires (Genesis 10:8-12).

Empires

One of the empires he founded was Nineveh that becomes the Assyrian empire. Both Babylon and Assyria are used by God to Judge the nation Israel. After King Solomon died Israel divided into two kingdoms. The northern is called Israel and the southern is called Judah.

God used Assyria to take Israel (northern kingdom) captive because of their sin and idolatry. He then uses Babylon, who conquered Assyria, to take the southern kingdom, Judah, captive for 70 years. Why 70 years? Judah failed to keep the sabbatical year of letting the land rest every 7th year. They did this for 490 years. God, being gracious, patient and merciful gave them 490 years to repent. They didn't. Therefore, God, being just, righteous and awesome, said, okay, after 490 years you owe me 70. That is why the captivity lasted for 7 decades.

Abraham

Hammurabi became the ruler of Babylonia (c. 2000—1600 B.C.) a few centuries after Nimrod. Approximately at this time Abraham left Ur, an ancient city in the southern part of Babylon, and moved north to Haran. Later, Abraham traveled to the land of Canaan, with the under-standing that God would make him the father of a great nation (Genesis 12). God did! Abraham is the father of the Jews and Arabs.

Nebuchadnezzar

Nebuchadnezzar defeated Egypt at the Battle of Carchemish in 605 BC (Jeremiah 46). With Egypt out of the way and with Assyrian power weakening Babylon becomes the world empire. Nebuchadnezzar then lays siege to the city of Jerusalem. In fact, He did this on three occasions:

1. 605 B.C.—this time he began bringing Jewish captives in throngs to
   Babylon, including Daniel (2 Kings 23:34-24:5; 2 Chronicles 36:5-8;
   Daniel 1:1-3)

2. 597 B.C.—More Jews taken to Babylon, this time including Ezekiel
   (2 Kings 24:6-16; 2 Chronicles 36:8-10)

3. 586 B.C.—He burned Jerusalem and destroyed the Temple (Lamenta-
   tions; 2 Chronicles 36:15-21; 2 Kings 25:1-21; Jeremiah 39)

Babylon Falls

Belshazzar, Nebuchadnezzar's grandson, eventually became king of
Babylon. Inviting 1,000 dignitaries with their wives and concubines to a
hedonistic banquet. Belshazzar brought the golden vessels out of storage
that his grandfather took from Holy Temple in Jerusalem. He filled them
with wine and offered a toast to the gods of gold, silver, brass, iron, wood
and stone (Daniel 5).

That same hour the God of heaven revealed an ominous message to
this wicked pagan king. The handwriting on the wall was very clear. King
Belshazzar, your kingdom is finished. You are weighed in the balances
and found wanting. Your kingdom is divided and given to the Medes and
Persians. Your time is up king.

That night the soldiers of Darius (Cyrus) the Persian were entering the
city. In the autumn of 539 B.C. during the drunken, hedonistic orgy
Babylon fell into the hands of the mighty Persians. Belshazzar, was slain
that very hour. A new empire now reigns.

The New Testament

Babylon is the only city mentioned in the Matthew's genealogy of the
Lord. Peter wrote his first epistle from Babylon around 65 A.D. (1 Peter
5:13). John mentions several times Babylon in the Book of Revelation.
Babylon has now become a synonym, a by-word, a proverb for the
antithesis of God and anything good and pure. Babylon is yet to play an

important role in the events of the last days and the rule of the Anti-Christ.

Today

1920   Until 1920 Iraq was part of the Ottoman Empire. On April 25, 1920 Iraq is placed under British mandate.

1921   Faysal, son of Hussein Bin Ali, the Sharif of Mecca, is crowned Iraq's first king.

1932   October 3, Iraq becomes an independent state.

1958   The monarchy is overthrown and Iraq is declared a republic and Abd-al-Karim Qasim becomes prime minister.

1963   February 8, Qasim is overthrown and Arif becomes president (Arab Socialist Baath Party).

1963   November 18, The Baathist government is overthrown by Arif and officers.

1966   Arif is killed in a helicopter crash, his brother, Maj-Gen Abd-al-Rahman Muhammad Arif, succeeds him as president.

1968   A Ba'thist led-coup ousts Arif and Gen Ahmad Hasan al-Bakr becomes president.

1979   President Al-Bakr resigns and is succeeded by Vice-President Saddam Hussein.

1980   Iran/Iraq war starts

1981   Israel attacks an Iraqi nuclear research center at Tuwaythah near Baghdad.

1988   Iraq uses chemical weapons against the Kurdish town of Halabjah.

1990   Iraq invades Kuwait.

1991   Gulf War I begins.

1994   Saddam Hussein becomes prime minister.

1995   Saddam Hussein's son-in-law, his brother, and their families, leave Iraq and are granted asylum in Jordan.

1996   Hussein's son-in-law and brother are promised a pardon, return to Baghdad, and are killed.

2003   UK's ambassador to the UN says the diplomatic process on Iraq has ended; UN Secretary-General orders the evacuation of arms inspectors from Iraq; US President George W. Bush gives Saddam Hussein and his sons 48 hours to leave Iraq or face war.

2003   March 20, American missiles hit targets in Baghdad, starting Gulf War II.

Above is simply a brief sketch of the recent history of Iraq. Gulf War II is uncovering the horrible atrocities of the evil regime of Saddam Hussein. Babylon is to play an important part in last day events, as we will see in the next section.

Future

There are two cities that are elevated in Scripture. Jerusalem, the city of God, and Babylon, the city of man. Both begin in Genesis and climax in the book of Revelation. One continues in glorious splendor for all eternity and the other ends in complete destruction.

There are 6 chapters that focus on Babylon in the last days:

- Isaiah 13,14—tells of the destruction of Babylon about a century before it becomes a power.

- Jeremiah 50,51—describes the destruction of Babylon. It is yet to happen.

- Revelation 17,18—also describes the destruction even to the point that it will cause the merchants of the world to mourn (Revelation 18:11)

Babylon was never destroyed. When the Persians became the world empire, they took Babylon without destroying it. However, this area will be destroyed, never to be inhabited again. As you study these 6 chapters of the Bible you will discover that Babylon plays an important role in the last days and in the government of the Anti-Christ.

Some Orthodox Jews believe that God will avenge Nebuchadnezzar's siege of Jerusalem and the taking the Temple treasuries, and destroying the Temple. Evangelicals believe that God's Word is true and will come to pass even if it takes millennia. Therefore, according to the Scriptures Babylon is to be destroyed. Many believe this has not yet happened. So do I.

The place that started out as Paradise ends horribly representing the antithesis of God. Perhaps, today's rebuilding of modern day Iraq is the beginning of creating an entity that will cause the world to mourn its loss, when it is finally destroyed.

God is in control of human events. He is preparing the world for events that are to come.

"And when these things begin to come to pass, then look up, and lift up your heads, for your redemption draweth nigh" (Luke 21:28).

20

The Roadmap for Peace?

The Palestinian Prime Minister, Mahmoud Abbas, is suppose to disengage the various terrorist groups Hamas, Islamic Jihad and Arafat's Al Aksa Brigades. These terrorists are those who strap bombs to their bodies and blow themselves up with the objective of killing and maiming Israelis, or, anyone else who stands in their way. The reason? They want Israel out of the land and pushed into the sea. They do not want Israel to exist.

Who Owns the Land?

The tension is over the land. Who owns this piece of real estate? To begin to understand who owns the land, we need to look at the first book of the Bible, the Book of Genesis.

> "*In the beginning God created the heaven and the earth*"
> (Genesis 1:1)

Why does the Torah* (Gr. Pentateuch*) start with God creating the world and the universe? You would think God would want to start the Bible with the first commandment that was given to Israel: *"This month shall be unto you the beginning of months" (Exodus 12:2)*. Why would

He choose to mention that He created the heaven and earth at the very outset?

The answer is found in Psalm 111:6. *"He hath shewed his people the power of His works, that He may give them the heritage of the heathen."*

The Hebrew word translated *"heathen"* can also be translated ("nations" or "Gentiles"). Therefore, God created the earth thus showing *"the power of His works"*, in order *"that He may give them* (Israel) *the heritage of the nations."*

So the entire world belongs to God. He created it, He fashioned it by His power. He spoke it into existence. It is His! As a result He can give it to whomever He wishes.

Legal Rights

The Scripture tells us that God took a certain piece of land, from the world He created, and gave it to Israel. O yes, He allowed other people to live there for a while. But when the time had come, He promised it and gave it to the descendants of Abraham through Isaac.

God is instructing (*Torah*) us from the very beginning of the Bible as to who owns the Land. God created it. Therefore, He owns it…and He gave it to Israel. Therefore, *Israel has a legal right to it.*

The Book of Genesis is a book of firsts or beginnings. God is teaching us concerning His first principles. This thought carries over throughout the whole of Scripture. *"The Lord possessed me in the beginning* (or first principle) *of his way, before His works of old" (Proverbs 8:22).*

God says of Israel, *"Israel was holiness unto the LORD, and the firstfruits of his increase* (or the beginning or first choice of His harvest or crop)*: all that devour him shall offend; evil shall come upon them, saith the LORD" (Jeremiah 2:3).*

God also says of Israel, *"This people have I formed* (created) *for myself; they shall shew forth my praise"* (Isaiah 43:21).

Therefore, the emphasis of Genesis chapter one is not only that God created the earth and the universe, but also, that because He created it, the land technically belongs to Him. And since it belongs to Him, He can give it to whomever He wishes. *So where is this land that was given to Israel?*

The Land Grant

The land promised to Israel is found in Genesis 15:18 and Ezekiel 48:1-29. Reading these verses you find that the land given to Abraham from God extends from the River of Egypt to the Great River Euphrates. From Hamath, near Damascus, to Kadesh in the south.

The inheritance of the land belongs to the Jews. So when will this take place? The fact the land was given to the Jews by God, and, that they would be scattered throughout the world until the last days, and then, return to the land is found throughout the Scripture. We learn that the return will be progressive (Ezekiel 37) and will culminate when Messiah comes and establishes His kingdom.

So when we pray for the *"peace of Jerusalem" (Psalm 122:6),* we are actually praying *"Thy Kingdom come. Thy will be done in earth, as it is in heaven" (Matthew 6:10).*

Will the Palestinian Prime Minister, the Israeli Prime Minister, Prime Minister Tony Blair and President George W. Bush bring lasting peace to Israel? Unfortunately no. ***There will be no peace until the Prince of Peace comes.***

Until then, Christians have a job to do. We must *pray for* Israel, *stand with* Israel and *share with them the hope* of their Messiah, the Lord Jesus.

- ***Torah*** is Hebrew meaning: *"law," "teaching"* or *"instruction."*

- ***Pentateuch*** is Greek meaning: *penta* ("five") and *teuchos* (papyrus rolls or scroll).

- Torah or Pentateuch refers to the first five books of the Bible written by Moses

About Dr. Jeffrey D. Johnson

Over 25 years of full-time ministry

Founder/Director of Israel Today Ministries

Director of tours to the Middle East

Senior Pastor in Ohio, Massachusetts and California

Almost 7 years directorship with International Ministries
to Israel (formerly, The American Association for
Jewish Evangelism, where the famed Hyman Appelman
was the first president)

Conference speaker

Bible Expositor

Guest lecturer

Author

Editor of the *"Research Review"*

Born and raised in the Midwest Dr. Johnson took his B.D. from Massillon Baptist College, his MA from Moody Bible Institute and his Th.M. and Th.D. from Christian Bible College. His passion for Israel, the Jewish roots of Christianity and Bible prophecy is well known.

His teaching will stir your heart to follow the Lord and to love and *"pray for the peace of Jerusalem"* (Psalm 122:6).

As an "Itinerant Bible Teacher" Dr. Johnson will travel anywhere to proclaim God redeeming Grace through our Lord and Savior Jesus the Messiah, *"to the Jew first, and also to the Greek"* (Romans 1:16).

His call is to "Teach the Church about Israel; Teach Israel about their Messiah; & to Feed and Clothe those in need (Genesis 12:3; Romans 15:27).

Dr. Jeff and his wife Louise have purposed to serve the Lord by going anywhere to teach the Bible to those desiring to know Him and His truth, trusting God to provide the funds and resources for their livelihood.

Israel Today Ministries, founded by Dr. Johnson, is a faith ministry, supported by "love offerings" from those interested in the ministry. Dr. Jeff and Louise have been commissioned and sent out by their home church.

Join Louise and me as we pray for the peace of Jerusalem and bless God's ancient people Israel. Partner with us as we teach the Church about Israel and Israel about their Messiah.

This is Daniel. His mommy cannot afford to buy food, let alone pay the electric bill. Living up in a fifth floor apartment he doesn't have much room to play and it gets cold at night. His mother was so appreciative of the food that was brought to her. Daniel took my heart. As I looked upon him, I was looking at Jesus. *"Inasmuch as ye have done it unto one of the least of these my brethren, ye have done it unto me." Matthew 25:40* Because of your gifts, Daniel will have food to eat tonight.

And I will bless them that bless thee, and curse him that curseth thee: and in thee shall all the families of the earth be blessed. Genesis 12:3

Pray for the peace of Jerusalem: they shall prosper that love thee. Psalm 122:6

Until He comes, we are
Together Under His Wings,

Dr. Jeffrey D. Johnson

ABOUT ISRAEL TODAY MINISTRIES

Three-fold Purpose:

Teach the Church about Israel

Teach Israel about Their Messiah

Help Feed & Clothe Those in Need
(Romans 15:27; Genesis 12:1-3)

To receive the *"Research Review"* Dr. Johnson's teaching newsletter, or if you would like to send a gift to Israel Today Ministries, or if you would like Dr. Johnson to speak at your church, event, school, or small group contact:

Israel Today Ministries
PO Box 522
Vista, CA 92085
Phone/Fax 760.643.CARE (2273)

෫ාඥ

COMMENTS FROM CHRISTIAN LEADERS

W hat others have said about the international ministry of Dr. Jeffrey Johnson:

I am pleased to recommend him to churches as an able expositor of the Word of God.

> — the late **John Walvoord**, Chancellor, Dallas Theological Seminary

A Bible Expositor with special insights on the origin, nature and destiny of God's chosen people, Israel.

> — **John C. Whitcomb**, Bible Scholar, Author, Professor

A careful expositor of Scripture.

> — **Homer Kent**, President Emeritus, Grace College and Seminary

A practitioner of all that he preaches.

— **Paige Patterson**, former President of the
Southern Baptist Convention, President of
Southeastern Baptist Theological Seminary

He has a wonderful grasp of Jewish history and liturgy.

— **Edgar C. James**, Professor, Moody Bible
Institute

*He is a person who has been uniquely prepared by God to
preach and teach about God's special people. Any one
who hears him will come away with a great love for the
people of Abraham.*

— **Dick Dahlquist,** Chair, Pastoral Studies,
Acting Dean, Grace College of Graduate
Studies

*He has a gifted teaching ministry which encompasses Biblical
prophecy and insights into modern-day Judaism.*

— the late **Paul Tassell**, Bible Scholar, Author,
former National Representative of G.A.R.B.C.

He has a great ministry.

— **LaVerne Butler**, former President of Mid-
Continent Baptist College, Scholar, Conference Speaker, President, Pulpit Aflame

Your heart will be thrilled as he ministers the prophetic Scriptures.

— the late **Alden A. Gannett**, President Emeritus of Southeastern Bible College, Bible Scholar, Author, Conference Speaker, President, Gannett Ministries

He loves the people and nation of Israel. He has given himself to a thorough study of God's ancient people and of the prophetic.

— *Ivan H. French, Pastor Emeritus, Pleasant View Bible Church, former Professor, Grace College and Seminary*